3

LIBRARY SERVICE

A 8029 00 054823

Books and discs must be returned on or before the last date stamped on label or on card in book pocket. Books or discs can be renewed by telephone, letter or personal call unless required by another reader.

For hours of opening and charges see notices at the above branch, but note that all lending departments close on Wednesday and Friday (p.m.) and all libraries are closed on Sundays, Good Friday, Christmas Day, Bank Holidays and Saturdays prior to Bank Holidays.

287

SELF DEFICIENCY

The Real Truth about Country Life

SELF DEFICIENCY

The Real Truth about Country Life

SALLY BORST

With line drawings by Sid Ponsford

DAVID & CHARLES
Newton Abbot London

British Library Cataloguing in Publication Data
Borst, Sally
Self deficiency.
1. (Republic) Ireland. Rural regions.
Households. Self-sufficiency
I. Title
640
ISBN 0-7153-9265-4

First published 1989
and printed in Great Britain
by Billings & Son Ltd, Worcester
for David & Charles Publishers plc
Brunel House Newton Abbot Devon

CONTENTS

To Pat and the children whom I love.

1

DROPPING OUT THE
HARD WAY

There is a growing tendency these days to return to the
country. To be at peace with everything and everybody
and live in total harmony with nature. Every magazine you
pick up is full of other people's country homes, complete
with log fires, chintzy wallpaper and gardens awash with
glorious flowers. Overhead the odd fleecy cloud nestles in
an azure sky and as you idly turn the pages, you will see
just what every well-dressed person is wearing down at
the farm these days. Deep down, maybe we all dream of
a better life, of something different to what we have got,
but few take the steps to find it.

But should you consider seriously getting away from it
all, there are a few ground rules worth consideration right
from the start – unless you want to be disappointed. The
first, foremost and most important of these is that idyllic
country lives don't depend on high ideals and brown rice,
they depend on MONEY. If you want what is in those

magazines, then find yourself the nearest millionaire to team up with. If, however, you are like us – with little money and lots of enthusiasm – you may think that the answer is self-sufficiency.

Self-sufficiency, by its very name, suggests that with your own two hands you can make a life for yourself. This is partly true. What you will find nearly impossible is making things like electricity, telephones, cars, etc. In other words, the material things that we so readily take for granted as being part of this 'life'. By 'getting away from it all', you probably don't mean taking yourself out to the nearest deserted space and plonking yourself down without food, shelter, and the family pets. The chances are you will want to retain the few basic fundamentals you have come to know and love over the years. Of course, you can sell up all you own and use this money to start your new life, but how do you support these basic fundamentals when it's all gone?

Self-sufficiency is what it says it is – it may just about support you, but it definitely won't supply any extra and it doesn't take into account the wife/husband and kids you may have that want to go along too. In other words, unless you are prepared to be equally self-sufficient, you will have problems. Now, it's possible to either overcome these or come to terms with them, one way or another. Either way, your new life will be a surprise. You are going to meet someone you have probably never come across before – THE REAL YOU. When there's nobody to impress, nowhere to get help from, no-one to scream at, just absolutely nobody at all, then is the moment you will find your own measure of self-sufficiency and, deficient as it is from your original plan, it could be exactly what you've been looking for.

Thinking back, neither Pat, my husband of five years, or myself had any particular intentions of starting a new life away from it all – it was more just a set of random

circumstances that all came together at once. He was thirty-two, an ex-merchant seaman and yours truly was thirty-three, a mum of two boys aged four and two and running a restaurant in the country pub of which we were tenants. In the dimmer past of Life-Before-Pat, someone had once referred to me as an entrepreneur. Having looked this up in the dictionary, it said that this is a person who organises, operates and assumes the risk for business ventures. That all sounds very grand and although there are hazy corners of my memory that recall jetting around the world, palm-fringed beaches and endless Beautiful People, it had come as quite a surprise to my somewhat jaded self, when meeting Pat we were both so totally bowled over by each other that we got engaged and married in the space of three months. Life was to prove not all roses however, mainly due to the fact that although Pat loved being mine-host in the pub, it came as something of a shock to me to find myself on the other side of the bar. Time was quickly to show me that there was nothing more horrible than trying to be nice to drunk people when you are sober and having our privacy constantly invaded with never a day off together.

With the arrival of Jason a year later and Mark two years after that came the nannies and mother's helps because every moment of the day was taken up with running the restaurant and just being a publican's wife in general. We couldn't even have a decent row together because it was always opening-time or closing-time or somebody-might-hear-us time. Slowly and imperceptibly, my temper was becoming like an unexploded bomb and after four years of wind-up, something had to give. That 'something' was my long-suffering husband Pat. Faced with this increasingly neurotic female and really just wanting a little peace and quiet instead of constant hassle, he agreed that we should give the brewery the statutory year's notice required to quit. A year seemed like plenty enough time to find another job, but even back in those days both of us had reckoned without a few basic home truths. Whereas I had been forced into a 'good' education and had various exams to my credit, Pat had left school at the age of fourteen to go to sea. His application forms for various jobs had large, blank spaces at the top where is said 'Further Education' and most of the potential employers he approached never bothered to turn over the page before rejecting him. The year seemed to speed by and there was nothing really on the horizon for us apart from a possible job with the Coastguards or for Pat to go back to sea, neither of which we wanted.

It was probably a touch of desperation that made Pat so enthusiastic that day when a lone Irishman wandered into the pub and during their conversation on fishing, happened to say what a marvellous deal the Irish Government had on fishing boats. A ninety per cent grant – could it be true? To keep the peace, a letter was hastily despatched to them and they duly wrote back and confirmed it was. By this time the full implication of having written at all was beginning to sink in as he constantly regaled me with stories of how marvellous Ireland was, how wonderful the people were and, most important of all, how great the fishing was. Now, my knowledge of fishing was limited to the odd childhood memory of going out to catch mackerel and my impression of Ireland was somewhat coloured by the news headlines of the past twenty years. But our tempers were so frayed at that point that, unable to face the possibility of an entire lifetime spent saying 'if only we had gone to Ireland, it would all have been different', in a quick rush of blood to the head and with more than usual vehemence, Pat was told to get himself off to bloody Ireland if it was so wonderful and, providing he could find himself a job and somewhere to live, then to give me a ring.

It was one of those occasions when you say something and then instantly regret having said it, but stubborn pride refused to let me beg him to change his mind about going and a few days later he set off up the road in our battered VW Beetle clutching a map of Ireland and his toothbrush. Some three weeks later, beginning to think that we would never hear from him again, the telephone call came. He had a job diving for sea-urchins (what were they?) and had rented a house for six months. My part in all this was to pack enough things to last us for that time, buy a self-sufficiency book, put the rest of the stuff into storage and come over on the following Tuesday. Our alternative lifestyle had begun.

Looking back, this was probably the best way to go. When, and if, you decide to do the same, you will find that all your loving relatives and friends suddenly step back and regard you in horror. You will be exposing those dear little children of yours to untold dangers. No matter which country you choose, it will suddenly be on the brink of total anarchy and everybody will have had at least three dreadful experiences there which they will relate to you in graphic detail. There are two pieces of advice worth mentioning at this point. The first is to go quickly without looking back and without regrets. The second is that at this stage you don't look too carefully at your new self-sufficiency book. There will be things in it that will be useful and things that definitely will not. This is because a quick flick through the pages can reveal such things as How to Slaughter Your Pig, How to Build a Farm Gate, Making Bricks and The Balfour Method of Rearing Chickens. At best it will confuse you, at worst, you will change your mind about the whole thing on the spot.

For me, there followed a few days of total chaos getting everything packed up and trying to decide what five persons would wear for six months. The self-sufficiency book had not mentioned clothing for beginners. With the benefit of hindsight, a great deal of trouble, packing and unpacking could have been avoided. But you, like me, will have absolutely no idea of what lies ahead and will only be able to base your ideas on what has gone before. If a dozen people had told me that we all would only need a couple of pairs of jeans, wellies and the odd sweater or shirt, none of us would ever have believed them, so the packing continued. We ended up at the ferryport with two small, rather bewildered children, a bearded collie dog called Pepper, an ancient cavalier King Charles spaniel called Taro, two cats, eleven suitcases, one overnight bag, one portable television and a boy's bicycle that Jason hysterically refused to let the men put into the storage lorry.

Also, just before locking up the pub for the last time, a persistent nagging feeling kept telling me that all was not as it should be and that something was definitely missing. With a sinking heart the full realisation of what that 'thing' was hit me. My period. In the turmoil and confusion of the last few weeks it had somehow escaped my notice, but now there was no doubt about it, I was quite definitely pregnant again. At this point you should recall that Pat was already in Ireland with the car whilst we were on the other side of the water without it. If the opportunity ever came my way to live to be a hundred, nothing will ever persuade me to make the journey from England to Ireland by boat again. Having obtained tranquillisers from the vet and given them to the two cats in their cage and to the two dogs on arrival at the ferryport, Taro promptly lay down and went to sleep on the spot. As Markie refused to crawl or walk and insisted on being carried, it became necessary for me to drag a sleeping spaniel on the lead behind me onto the ship.

It would have been a far better idea to take all the tranquillisers myself. The dogs, cats, bicycle, TV and suitcases were put in one part of the ship by the friend who had brought us up to Swansea, and myself, the overnight bag and the children taken to a cabin which must have been inside the main engine, judging from the noise and the heat. Trying to save money by thinking I could fit in a

bunk with two-year-old Markie was another big mistake. By 4.00am and verging on desperation, there was nothing left for me but to swallow down most of Markie's teething medicine which warned in large letters on the label that it might cause drowsiness in a three year old. Falling fitfully asleep by about half past four, two and a half hours later we docked in Cork. It took me nearly an hour to organise myself and the children and find our way up to the main deck and the way off. From our floating vantage point, we could see that there was no sign of Pat or the car in the car-park (Pat is one of those people who will be late for his own funeral) and, on making enquiries as to the whereabouts of our other luggage, cats, dogs etc, I was told in no uncertain terms to find them myself. With two small children, one of whom was at the crawling stage and one who was fascinated with what was going on over the edge of the rails, there was no way I was going to start an in-depth search of the ship, so sticking out my nearly two-month pregnant stomach as far as possible, I told the purser that if they didn't help me, we would all just have to sail backwards and forwards with the ship until such time as they did. We then sat firmly down on the deck, kids and all, to add emphasis to our protest. It wasn't long before six burly sailors arrived with all our bits and pieces and practically threw us off bodily into the customs hall. It really wasn't the fault of the poor customs man that he happened to pick on us for a search, it was probably just the suddeness of our arrival, but having everything unpacked again was just about the last straw. I was about to tell him his fortune in no uncertain terms, when thankfully Pat showed up and prevented a great deal of trouble for us all by explaining our situation. Though still grumpy and more than a little sleepy, we were delighted to see him and to hear that he had arranged for another car to come up from a place called Kenmare to help with the luggage and take us all back to where we were to live. Excitedly chatting about all the

news he had missed during his time away, especially the bit about his prospective fatherhood, we walked the dogs and then sat down on the pavement outside the ferryport to await the arrival of the other car.

Some four hours later, as we were just beginning to think that maybe the relatives had been right, the car showed up towing what looked and smelled like a recently occupied cattle trailer, and all our luggage, plus the cats still in their cage were loaded into it. Pat, myself, the two children and the two dogs squashed into the Beetle and saying that we would all meet up at the house Pat had rented, we set off. What we did not know at this point was that the other driver planned to spend the day in Cork before making the journey back down.

My first impressions of Ireland were seen through a tired haze, but we couldn't fail to gasp in amazement at the beauty of the golden and brown mountains that marked the borders of Cork with Kerry and the high hedges dripping with scarlet fuchsia that lined each side of the road. About one and a half hours travelling brought us to the town of

Kenmare where the Kenmare River broadens out to meet
the Atlantic Ocean and about half an hour after that we
arrived at our rented house.

Located at the start of the Beara Peninsula, about as
far south-west as you can go before you fall into the sea –
next stop the USA – the whitewashed cottage overlooked
the most magnificent views of the towering Caha mountains, the entrance to Killmackillogue Bay and the part of
the Kenmare River whose far shores rise up to become
the winding roads and hills of The Ring of Kerry. It's a
sight that even now still takes my breath away. You could
stand at the cottage door and on a still day hear the plop
of the gannets as they plummeted into the water nearly
half a mile away, such was the total stillness. Feeling a
great deal happier at the sight of all this beauty, we went
on into the cottage.

My happiness proved to be shortlived. If there was a
prize given for the coldest cottage in Ireland, this would
have won it hands down! Although a pretty, typically Irish
whitewashed cottage on the outside, that was not the case
on the inside. Somebody had run amuck making the whole
place open-plan. They had got rid of all those nasty little
rooms with their tiny windows and the big fireplaces and
installed electric central heating, large windows, practically no interior walls and a small, two-foot square fireplace
that wouldn't be nasty and messy and wasteful like those
big ones. It was, in other words, a typical holiday home
in which the owner had obviously never spent an Irish
winter. There is an excellent reason why the Irish have
always built cottages the way they do and we were about
to find it out. However, as the autumn days shortened into
winter, we were too entranced by the sheer beauty of the
surroundings and the novelty of our new way of life to
worry about it at all.

Pat had been given a job by a man who bought sea-
urchins, the edible variety. He gave Pat all the diving gear

he needed and lots of cardboard boxes. Pat had to get his own boat and a compressor (to refill the air tanks), dive down, get the sea-urchins, bring them back in, pack them in the boxes and sell them to the man. It sounded simple. Pat was an experienced diver and he worked out that if he dived for six hours a day, in a few months we could all be filthy rich. He then spent most of our capital on the deposit for a Zodiac inflatable boat and engine, bought a second-hand compressor and put this in the kitchen.

Now, if like me, you have never shared a kitchen with a compressor, it is likely to come as something of a shock. The noise it makes is quite overwhelming, causing the walls to shake, your head to shake and generally to render any conversation or cooking impossible. So he moved it into a nearby shed. My job was to keep an eye on the tanks that were filling (which then entailed standing in the shed instead of the kitchen for most of the day) and when they were full, to take them down to him. As he was under the water, this was a little difficult. You had to look for the bubbles and when you found them, you could lob the odd stone in the water and hope that if it missed him he would notice it and come up to the surface. Finding bubbles on a choppy day was like looking for a needle in a haystack. Wandering miles along rocky beaches carrying two full diving tanks nearly killed me, but it was nothing to packing up the urchins at the end of the day.

These delightful little sea creatures closely resemble a dark purple hedgehog. Frenchmen, it would seem, have a penchant for their roe (eggs, to you and me) which are sort of pink and watery and supposed to be a violent aphrodisiac. As we could never bring ourselves to try them, we never got to find out if it was really true. If you are nasty to a sea-urchin, it shoots its roe out all over the place and, if it is out of the water at the time, it then dies. It is very easy to be nasty to a sea-urchin, especially when you have packed several hundred of them into boxes and got most of their long, sharp spines in your fingers. You get so many in your fingers because you have to pack them on the beach in the dark, so that the dear little things don't get upset by being hauled around in sacks. A description of what they smell like is unnecessary. Suffice to say it wouldn't upset me too much if I never see another one as long as I live.

The Indian summer continued for about a month, and then, one morning winter arrived. We awoke to find the whole cottage shuddering against the blast of the first gales, and by half past nine had to open the windows at the back of the house to stop the wind lifting the roof up. This was because the new windows at the front didn't fit properly and most of the gales were swirling around the open-plan. Obviously Pat couldn't dive. Forays were made out to the beach to haul the inflatable up even higher, attempts were made to dry out our clothes and ourselves, and we consoled each other with the thought that it couldn't last.

Six weeks later the wind was still howling. Our finances were going from bad to terrible, and most of our money went into the ever-hungry electric meter trying to keep warm. Eventually, in December the weather broke and the sun shone weakly over the frosty landscape. It got colder and colder and how Pat ever dived into that green, icy water for up to five·hours at a time is beyond me, but all the fresh water brought down by the storms into the sea had killed many of the sea-urchins and it became necessary to go further and further afield to look for them. Being five month's pregnant, it was becoming more and more difficult to haul the air tanks around, plus two small children. Still the temperature continued to drop, until one morning the fresh water on the surface of the sea froze and Pat was having to break the ice to dive in. In four short weeks he dropped two stone in weight. From never having had a sweet tooth, he now got pre-natal cravings for treacle puddings and the like, in a desperate attempt to keep up his strength for the diving so we could replenish our practically empty coffers.

The prospect of Christmas seemed dismal. But we had reckoned without our friends and neighbours. Six people promptly invited themselves for Christmas Day lunch, one couple brought a turkey, one couple brought a Christmas pudding and the last couple brought some wine. All we had to provide were the vegetables. The children persuaded a local farmer to let us have a fir tree and we made all kinds of decorations for it out of silver discarded sweetie papers that we found, berries, nuts and biscuits. On Christmas Eve another neighbour came round with some fairy lights to wind amongst the branches. Of all the trees in all the Christmases both before and after this one, none will ever be as magical as that one we had for our first Irish Christmas.

As Pat had only rented the cottage for six months, a lot of my time had also been taken up with looking for somewhere more permanent for us to rent and get down to some serious self-sufficiency. With the passing weeks the hopelessness of my task became more and more evident.

There were masses of empty cottages, bungalows, houses etc, but they were all for summer letting only. Many of these were owned by Europeans and only occupied for a couple of weeks a year. The rest of the time they sat empty and forlorn. Trying to explain to the owners of an Irish cottage that if they let it to us at a lower rent over a longer period this would result in them getting the same amount of money, was a waste of time. Also, we had all our furniture in storage in England and wanted somewhere unfurnished. In desperation we looked at abandoned and derelict cottages, but the majority of these either had no running water or no electricity. We couldn't stay where we were, even if we had wanted to, because it too was already let for the summer tourist season and we had instructions to be out by the end of March, so it was beginning to look as if the baby would be born in a tent.

Then, just when things seemed as though they couldn't get any worse, the urchin-buyer went broke. The diving suit and gear had to be returned to be sold and we were left with a boat we couldn't pay for and no income at all. First the compressor had to go, then the boat, and we had to live on what they called Supplementary Welfare of £28.00 a week. Supplementary to what was never made quite clear. During those days we lived on a most peculiar diet consisting of either porridge or rice. This was often accompanied by an assortment of seafood and shellfish found along the sea shore. We ate mussels from the rocks, scallops from the beach at low tide and *clúaisín* (a sort of black, tiny queen scallop), and we fished from the shore for the occasional passing mackerel or pollock. For vegetables we ate turnips and cabbage given to us by neighbours, plus an abundance of potatoes. This was our first real experience of the generosity of the Irish. Our nearest physical neighbour was nearly a mile away, but it didn't seem to matter. With very little fuss and hardly ever identifying themselves as the donor, we would come home to find a leg of venison, or a sack of potatoes on the doorstep. At the local pub down in Killmakilloge harbour we were made to feel quite welcome and more often than not, Joan would declare that she just happened to have five dinners that needed eating up. The generosity and kindness of the local people to us at that time was to form a bond that will last a lifetime.

2

FAIRIES, FROGS AND
FOND FAREWELLS

One wet and windy morning in late March, a neighbour
dropped in for a chat and happened to mention an empty
cottage, not far from where we presently lived, that he
thought was available for rent. The only setback to it that
he knew of was that it had the reputation of being haunted
by the Fairies. He was so serious when he said it, that it
only seemed polite not to laugh aloud, but it didn't take
us long to fetch the keys and go round to see it. Haunted
or not, this looked like it could be the answer to all our
prayers. It was a little white cottage of the two-up/two-
down variety set right into the side of the mountain. The
road to Kenmare ran directly in front of the door, and on
the other side of the road the land plunged steeply down to
the sea. From the front door the view was quite spectacular
over the Kenmare River and the MacGillycuddy's Reeks,
with the snow-capped peaks of Carrauntoohill Mountain
towering over them all in the distance. We had been told

that thirty-six acres of land went with the cottage and, from what we could see, this had to be all the land up behind the house and all the land down in front of it.

The cottage itself had walls over a foot thick and more in places and an attempt had been made at some point in time to 'modernise' it. This meant that a lean-to kitchen had been put on the back of the building so that the outside wall of the kitchen actually touched the side of the mountain, making the windows level with the ground. The two halves of the house had obviously been separate at one time as each downstairs room had its own steep staircase up to a bedroom. One of these was an attic bedroom and the ceiling so low that it wasn't possible for Pat or me to stand upright, but the other was a fair size, with tiny windows at floor level all overlooking the spectacular view. Between the two halves, downstairs a bathroom had been built complete with bath and loo and handbasin. If there was a bath, there had to be water! An investigation up the side of the garden revealed a plastic pipe descending from somewhere up the mountain, ending up in a large black plastic water tank, and from this a pipe running down to the house. To cap it all, there was even electricity laid on!

Each downstairs room had a large fireplace. The man who had given us the keys had warned us that the living-room one smoked, but the one in the other room quite took our breath away. Over eight feet across, it had all the blackened blocks and tackle for roasting something as large as a pig, plus a swing-out crane from which hung two black cauldrons and an ancient kettle. The floors were concrete and there were the odd puddles of water around, but as we had been told that no-one had lived here for six years, that seemed acceptable. The furniture, such as it was, consisted of a few chairs, one table, two mattresses of a somewhat damp nature on the floors upstairs and sacks over the windows instead of curtains. An electric cooker of dubious age stood in the kitchen and a few odd knives and forks were the sum total of the fixtures and fittings.

Back outside, although it was a little odd to have trees growing above the level of the roof, there were enough of them around to give some shelter from the wind and even a few old gnarled apple trees were scattered here and there. And everywhere around there were lots of tiny little walls no more than a foot high which Pat suggested were probably to keep out the fairies. There were two sheds in various stages of neglect. One had no roof, and the other had a roof, but no door. It was inside the second one of these that we found an old signpost with the name of the house carved upon it. '*Fairy Pass*' it said.

It caused quite a stir down at the pub when we enquired further into the background and history of '*Fairy Pass*', along with the muttering and mumblings generally of a discouraging nature. It would seem that the cottage had been built not only in the middle of a Fairy Road, but also on a Fairy Ring. One was bad enough, two meant disaster. We heard stories of how the last two lots of encumbants had fled the house terrified in the middle of the night, never to return – hence why it had remained unoccupied for so long. There were tales of unexplained noises, moanings and general hauntings, culminating in the quite definite fact that it was not possible to shut any outside door in the house, as these always had to remain open for the fairies to pass through. It was this last and heavily emphasised fact that had given the house its name, to stand as a warning to all till the ends of time.

Not being one generally to believe too much in ghoulies and ghosties, fairies and the like, Pat was heard to remark that he thought any self-respecting fairy would move over to the other side of the river rather than share a house with our kids, but the children and I were not quite so sure, especially when we found out that fairies were not the pretty, nice, little things with wings that we had been

reared on, but were, in fact, the souls of the dead who were
unable to rest in peace – in other words, ghosts. But it was
a house, it was charming and it was available, so we rang
the owner who lived in America and arranged to move in
immediately.

Now, there are a few points that you should take note
of here before going any further. If, unlike us, you are
lucky enough to have a choice of homes, never be bowled
over by its external beauty and charm. Be practical. Take
note of those puddles on the floor – ask yourselves, where
do they come from? If there are no holes in the roof,
they must have come from elsewhere. If the house is on
a mountainside, anything coming down the mountain will
either pass through, over or under it, and for goodness
sake, rush outside with a garden fork and see if you plunge
it into the soil to more than a depth of two inches before
hitting bedrock, because the soil on most mountains long
since washed away down to the sea. And finally, take a
look and see if you can see the sun. This was particularly
important in our case because we were to find out that for
the six winter months of the year, ie September to March,
the sun was never to come around our side of the mountain,
leaving us in gloom and shade and always shining gloatingly
on the other side of the river. We were to spend the next
five and half years of our lives here in this little cottage,
until our rapidly growing children forced us to look for
a bigger house. This time we had the benefit of hindsight
with which to conduct our search.

But it was late March now and the whole countryside
was filled with the urgency of spring's arrival. Each day
was spent scrubbing and cleaning and painting in an effort
to get the cottage habitable. Ancient, very cross spiders
had to be ousted by Pat or Jason as picking one up was
quite beyond me, and we made a big effort to remove or
disguise the very obvious damp on the walls. During the
unoccupied years, a great number of woodlice had moved

in and under most things in the house. Worst of all were the slugs. There's nothing quite so off-putting as finding an enormous fat slug halfway up the wall when you have just got in the bath! These were our first meetings with Kerry slugs which seemed to be twice as big and twice as slimy as any variety previously encountered. Being ignorant of such matters, it had never crossed my mind that slugs lived anywhere else except outside in the garden, and even years later it is still a mystery to me why a slug should choose to live indoors.

The ones that lived outdoors were obviously quite delighted with the sight of me rushing round planting seeds here and there. Although it was late spring and we hadn't yet found any soil deep enough to plant vegetables in, there was no reason why we couldn't have the place awash with flowers, just like all those marvellous magazine pictures. Out of the eighteen packets of seed planted, not one came up. Each one was set upon as it sprouted, and demolished. This was probably the first time it really became necessary to get out, dust off and consult the self-sufficiency book for advice. In order to trap slugs (did we really want to trap them? What should we do with it once we had trapped it?), one must place basins of beer or milk and water in the ground, the theory being that all the slugs will then rush headlong into them and drown. As we couldn't afford to be filling basins with beer specially for slugs, it was necessary to rely on the milk and water method, but obviously Kerry slugs are of the alcoholic variety. It was a dismal failure. It may not be very organic, but there is really only one way to control slugs, and that is with slug pellets, but by the time we found this out it was far too late to plant anything else.

It's hard to recall exactly when the realisation dawned on me that planting cultivated flowers was totally unnecessary out here. It must have been when, on checking my slug traps one morning, the question of why the slugs were so keen on my seeds and hadn't touched the millions of wild flowers that were carpeting the ground occurred to me. On actually opening my eyes and looking around me, the sheer profusion of colour and form was almost beyond belief. In a part of the world where agricultural chemicals are hardly ever used on the fields, Nature has been left to herself and can really show everybody what she is, and always has been, capable of. Out for a walk, the children would rush around gathering handfuls of fuchsia flowers to play with and we became fascinated with learning all the names of the wild flowers. There were ox-eye daisies, red campions and seas of yellow buttercups. The woods were full of delicate wood anemones, bluebells and greeny-yellow wood spurge. Broom as yellow as the sun was everywhere and the hedges were filled with blackberry blossom, honeysuckle and dog roses in pink and white. Vetch of every colour and hue twined in amongst the tall grasses, and pink mallow and sweet-smelling violets pushed up between the cowslips and primroses.

Down on the seashore the rocks looked pink from

a distance and further investigation would reveal them covered with thrift, whilst willowherb pushed its way up between the pebbles and the shells. There was always great excitement when we thought we had discovered a new and rare species and somebody would be sent to fetch the wild flower book, only to discover that it was called common butterwort or somesuch. On returning home from a walk one morning, there was an orchid nestling in the grass on the side of the road. Rushing home in a frenzy of excitement it wasn't long before it was dug up and carefully replanted outside the house. Having nurtured it with masses of tender, loving, care for simply ages, my attempts at conservation sustained quite a knock when Pat took me a short way up the mountain one day and showed me about an acre of beautiful orchids growing there! For the first time in my life it wasn't possible to utter a single complaint about never being given any flowers. The boys noticed Pat bringing me home the odd bunch he had found by the wayside, and from then on every available jam jar and container was filled with their offerings. So it seemed only sensible to stop worrying about the slugs and concentrate on other things.

By the end of April the furniture had arrived and shortly after that, Gemma Pauline Borst also made her appearance on 1 May. A healthy 8lb 4oz baby with a pair of lungs designed to keep us all on our toes. There had been no sign of fairies except for finding the front door wide open on our first morning in the house, but we had put that down to forgetfulness and the boys had long since demolished all the little walls around the house. They quickly became adept at leaping around on the side of the mountain and it wasn't long before they were bringing home shells and stones from the beach, and beetles and tadpoles from the many streams that rushed and swirled and chattered their way down the mountain.

It was about this time that we also made a few discoveries on the subject of water when one morning nothing came out of the tap. The tank seemed to be OK, so we started to follow the black plastic pipe back up the mountainside to its source. Now you will discover that the words 'gravity feed' when applied to a water supply, mean that the source of the water is somewhere very high up. If, like me, you get vertigo when standing on anything higher than a milk crate, you will discover why somebody invented plumbers. These must have originally been fearless mountain men with the feet of mountain goats and the grip of a limpet. This became obvious on finding that the pipe ascended vertically up the steepest slopes of the mountain, and we had to haul ourselves upwards by grabbing handfuls of bracken and slipping and sliding on the rocks, causing small landslides to rush down the mountain behind us.

On reaching what appeared to be the summit, I found to my dismay that we were only about half-way up and the pipe disappeared into a small, muddy pool. We cleared out as much of the pond weed and general debris as was possible and pulled baby frogs and tadpoles away from the end of the pipe where they were being sucked to their doom. It all looked highly unhygienic but Pat reasoned that most of the muck would settle in the bottom of the tank when it got there and weren't we all still alive and healthy? Despite any reservations you may have, it is probably quite wise to accept sensible, reasonable arguments like this and not dwell too finely on logic. In most remote country areas like this one, you are considered lucky to have any water supply at all. Mains services do not exist and the only alternative is to drill for water which is extremely costly.

All of us were to make that journey up the mountain to the water source many times in all kinds of weather, only to discover that a passing cow or goat had trodden on the pipe and pulled the joint apart, always just on the steepest bit. Joining two pieces of pipe together perched on a precipice with the water still gushing out of one end is a wet, thankless task at the best of times. You can always

console yourself with the lovely view – if you can pluck up the courage to look straight ahead and not down – and you can bet any amount of money that as soon as you get up there, somebody will come to call down at the house and never hear your frantic screamings to attract their attention from the summit.

The other aspect of plumbing that was to gain our attention fairly rapidly was the fact that only one of the pipes from the fixtures inside the house actually led anywhere. This, thankfully, was the one from the loo to the cesspit. Others such as the outlet pipes from the sink in the kitchen or from the bath went as far as the outside wall and then stopped. We were told on enquiry that this was the 'soakaway' system, though quite how the water was supposed to soakaway uphill was another matter entirely. What in fact happened was that when the water reached the outside wall, it promptly turned around and came back in again, not necessarily via the pipe. Pat found this out after he had taken a pickaxe to the ground outside the bathroom in an effort to determine exactly why the floor was always covered by about two inches of water. As we had absolutely no idea where the cesspit was and as laying pipes in the bedrock of the mountain seemed virtually impossible, we compromised by joining all the other pipes into the pipe that went from the loo to the cesspit and, thankfully, this seemed to work.

This was to be the first time that it became necessary for Pat to assume the role of a plumber. We were soon to learn that in order to survive here, you also had to become an electrician, a garage mechanic and a general repair man. It also helped to have a working knowledge of veterinary skills, medical skills, chimney sweeping and forestry. It is worth noting also that any ideas you might have about such tasks being 'man's work' or 'woman's work' soon go right out of the window. This particular lesson was to come home to me sooner rather than later.

Although Pat had attempted to get himself a permanent job on many occasions out here, we had learned that beautiful scenic places like this provided mainly seasonal work catering for the tourists. Even if we had still had the money, the amazing grant on fishing boats had been discontinued practically on the day we arrived. One of the jobs that Pat had applied for before we had left England was for a government-run course on oil rigs. I can't recall the precise reason why, but it never came to anything, so it was with some surprise that we received a letter, forwarded on by Grandma to us, stating that Pat should attend an interview in Oxford for the course. With Gemma recently born making an extra mouth to feed, it seemed daft not to take them up on it, so we scraped together enough money for the boat fare and all waved him a fond farewell. Had either of us known then that there were 11,000 applicants for this oil-rig course and only thirteen places on it, or that we were not to see each other again for sixteen weeks, the chances are that he never would have gone.

But go he did, and it was left to me to wend my way home from the ferryport in Cork, the Beetle piled high with the kids. Having driven about ten miles and just successfully negotiated central Cork, we were stopped by the Garda (the Irish police) and informed that my car had no lights at the back. To be truthful, this was the least of the Beetle's problems. She had been in an advanced state of decay before we left England, but after an Irish winter the salt-laden air and the numerous pot-holes in the road had brought her near to death. Pat had spent many hours before he left lying in the mud beneath her, Volkswagen manual in hand, doing the wheel bearings or somesuch, but he hadn't mentioned anything about lights. To be fair to the Garda, it had probably been a trying evening for him too, but it was nothing compared to what greeted him on looking in the window. Both boys were still crying their eyes out at the sudden departure of their dad, and Gemma, who thought it was obviously the done thing, had joined in and was screaming at the top of her very clamorous voice. He told me to pull into the nearest garage and then proceeded personally to buy and install the fuses for the lights and hasten me on my way again – probably delighted to have so easily gotten rid of this carload of wailing banshees. By the time we reached home some two hours later and I had got all the kids, bathed and bedded, I was too exhausted to contemplate the fact that my life as a part-time grass widow had begun.

3

FUEL, FIRES AND FLOODS

Whilst Pat stayed in the UK working his way through the
six different interviews, three in Oxford and then three in
Scotland, it was left to me to get on with the business of
living without a man around the place. To my dismay, it
soon became evident that somehow the routine jobs of the
day had fallen into the 'his' and 'her' categories. In the
former list, one of these was chopping the wood for the
two voracious fires in the house. We had managed to find
enough money to have a tractor load of wood delivered to
the yard, but it had to be split and then carried into the
house to dry out. It obviously wasn't exactly 'seasoned'
wood as most of it still had branches with leaves growing
vigorously out of them. Maybe if it had been, it might have
been easier to split, but this was my first time with an axe
in hand and you can take it from me that it isn't as easy
as you think.

My biggest problem was actually hitting the log at all,
let alone in the same place twice and fifteen minutes later
nothing much had been achieved except for me becoming a

sweaty, exhausted wreck. My good humour was not helped by Jason who sat nearby telling me how Daddy did it with one hand and could chop any size required. Eventually, by sending out the children to collect sticks for starter wood and by my hit and miss method, we got enough for the day. It soon became apparent that the trick was to get a small fire going really well and then just launch a couple of big logs on it and the fire will do the rest of the work. Firelighters, preferably bought in bulk, are an absolute must for the beginner, as it takes an awful lot of heat to get damp, green wood burning at all, and any thoughts about lazing in an armchair in the evening go out of the window when you discover that you have to get up every thirty minutes to check and see how the fires are going.

Now, in order to prevent the fire in the living-room from smoking, Pat had built up the hearth with stones and raised the level of the fireplace by about a foot. This seemed to work and definitely reduced the smoke in the room to a point where one could live with it. However, one gusty morning in July there was a knock at the door and a neighbour informed me that my chimney was on fire. As he was on his way home from church, several other volunteers followed and attempted to put the fire out. Because the chimney was above the level of the water tank, the hose pipe attached to the tap would not flow, so it meant buckets of water being scooped up out of the tank and then relayed up to the man on the roof, who in turn emptied them down the chimney. In no time at all the fire was out, cups of tea were made and thanks given all round for their prompt and efficient help.

Afterwards the children and I surveyed the damage. Twenty buckets of water emptied down your chimney into the grate doesn't do much for the decor of the room, but even worse was my fear of lighting the fire again in that room. There had been general agreement during the rescue that the cause of the blaze was raising the level of the hearth too far and not sweeping the chimney. On ten-tatively enquiring how one contacted the chimney sweep, it became apparent from the general hilarity that no such being existed and one did it oneself with a gorsebush. This seemed far too Heath Robinson for me, so, deciding to leave it to Pat to sort out on his return, it seemed that the best thing would be to just abandon the living-room and move the chairs into the other downstairs room that we were using as a dining-room.

We were soon to discover that having a fireplace eight feet across may have looked very rural and wonderful, but unless you had a fire in it eight feet across, anything smaller had very little effect on the room. It looked pretty, but all the heat went straight up the chimney and whilst it was going up there, it dragged the air from the rest of the house with it. Now, as the window frames didn't fit per-fectly, the end product was a roaring draught throughout the house, whilst we all sat practically inside the fireplace trying to keep warm. But it was summer time and we didn't need a fire until the evening and surely Pat would be back soon?

He, meanwhile, had got through all six interviews and been accepted for the course along with twenty-three others. This began just two weeks later, so it wasn't worth him coming back for that time, especially in view of the fact that he had gone over on a one-way ticket and we didn't have enough money for the return journey, let alone back again. But we were delighted with his success and were so busy wishing him well on the phone down at the pub that the fact of the course lasting another six weeks didn't really sink in till morning. Then the only thing foremost in my mind was the dismal thought of another six weeks of wood chopping and it was probably my despair at this that persuaded me to let Jason have a go with the axe. Trying not to think too hard of the consequences of letting a six year old loose with a full-sized axe, it soon became apparent that he was far more successful than me. In no time at all, we had a nice pile of split logs. Mind you, it was a bad mistake on his part, because he suddenly found himself with yet another job.

About this time the car died. Every time we took her out, more and more things seemed to go wrong and eventually one day on the way to Kenmare, she stopped never to go again. Although we were able to get her towed home, the general opinion was that she was beyond all help and the fact had to be faced that if we wanted to go anywhere from now on, we would have to either walk or hitch-hike. There was only one bicycle belonging to Jason that we had brought with us from England, so the children and myself did an awful lot of walking, most of which was done in the rain. This was because, although Jason would happily walk the two miles down to the pub (to get the milk and to visit the shop that seem to be an integral part of every Irish pub), Markie definitely would not. He was too large and heavy to fit in the pram with Gemma, especially going uphill on the way home, but we accidentally discovered that he loved to run and jump in puddles. So if you went out when it was raining, he would run along jumping from one puddle to the next and thus huge distances would be accomplished.

On these enforced walks, we would sing nursery rhymes and hold competitions as to who could pick the biggest bunch of wild flowers or gather the most blackberries, or find the most unusual stone, etc. Unbeknown to us, we were also discovering a whole new world that we had never seen from inside our car. We began to get familiar with what was growing where, noticing things like the wild plums on the trees and seeing how fast they were ripening and where the caches of small crimson wild strawberries hid themselves. Instead of confining ourselves to just our own bit of land around the house, suddenly we had a whole new territory out there that became just as familiar as if it had been our own garden. It seemed to me that this was really our first introduction to having our lives governed by the seasons of the year instead of the dates on a calendar. Although we all missed Pat dreadfully, it somehow helped not to count the days and our little expeditions down to the pub or up to the post office definitely drew me and the children closer together as we began to make small inroads into this wonderful, magical world of nature that before we had admired, but never really come close to.

The summer days lengthened into autumn. Pat completed his course with flying colours and we were simply delighted to hear from him that he had a job as a roustabout with a drilling company in Aberdeen which he could start immediately. He would definitely be back in four weeks, and with a pay cheque! Any ideas the locals had that all people who work on oil rigs must be millionaires were soon to be dispelled. Although in those days his pay was not bad, he worked four weeks on and four weeks off and he didn't get paid for the weeks he didn't work. So each pay cheque had to last us for eight weeks. Then, because he was working in the UK, he was on the PAYE system and had to donate a large portion (ie nearly half) of his pay to Mrs Thatcher's upkeep. For some reason best known to HMG he was taxed on emergency tax as a single man with no dependants. Being the only typist in the family, the job of taking up correspondence with the Tax Man was relegated to me, but it took several years and many letters to sort out. They didn't seem to have a slot or a form for people living in Ireland and working in the UK and commuting from one to the other. But although having a regular pay cheque made a great deal of difference to us, by this time we wouldn't swap our lifestyle for all the tea in China and it gave us the reassurance that we could now continue it.

When Pat eventually got home again, he was faced with not only the death of the car, but also shortly after his return, our ancient cavalier King Charles spaniel died.

Aged over sixteen, his life had been good and full, but it wasn't without a few tears that he was gently buried high up on the mountainside to gaze across the beautiful view into eternity. This was then followed by Pat having to attend to all those little jobs which had been put by for him. The first and most important one was the fireplace and the chimney in the living-room. He made enquiries as to how to clean it, and was told to get a small gorse bush and tie a rope to each end of it. Place the gorse bush inside the top of the chimney, with one rope going down inside it and the other down the outside of the house. One person then pulls the gorse bush down the chimney from inside and then the other person pulls it back up again from outside. Now, this definitely works, but you must remember to bear in mind the most important word of the whole operation, and that is 'small'. If, like us, you take a rough look at the size of the chimney and then cut a bush approximately the same size, you are quite likely to end up with a gorse bush down your chimney forever. That is because it's no trouble at all to pull it down the chimney. The problems come when you've got it about three quarters of the way back up again and it reaches the place where the chimney narrows before emerging into the chimney pot. Gorse bushes are not designed to shrink in small spaces and if it hadn't been for the fact that Pat is quite a strong lad, it would still be there. Anyway, by the time we got it out again and then up and down a few more times (with an appropriate number of branches removed), the chimney appeared quite clean from what we could see and Pat was sure it wasn't necessary to lower the level of the hearth.

That evening, as we held a small supper for some friends to celebrate Pat's return, with a rush and a roar, up went the chimney again, just as we were about to tuck into the main course. This is when we experienced the second method of chimney cleaning and that is to let it burn itself (and all the soot) out. This does require

extensive monitoring of things like making sure that the
joists in or near the chimney don't get too hot and set
the floorboards alight, removing all the children in case
they do, and calming down an upset wife who not only
has her dinner ruined, but is sure the whole house will
just be a pile of ashes in the morning. There is absolutely
no way this method could possibly be recommended for
the faint hearted. On awakening the next day to the
sound of bangs and crashes, I came down to find Pat
lowering the stones in the fireplace by a good six inches
and this combined with the spotless chimney solved the
smoking problem, unless of course, the wind was in the
wrong direction!

Living, as we were, by the sea, the wind is something
you have to get used to. Sooner rather than later. At best
it is a constant gentle breeze; at worst it's a howling gale
seeming to come from all directions at once. On windy
days you will discover all those little nooks and crannies
that give your cottage that outward 'olde-worlde' look as
it moans and shrieks through them. You just get them all
stuffed up with newspaper and the like, when the wind is
sure to change direction and you will discover lots more.
It will have a somewhat strange effect on your decor, but
you will learn to live with it when you discover that
everyone else has newspaper stuffed in the corners of their
windows and round the back door. You will also discover
that alongside clothes-pegs for the washing line, there are
also things called storm-pegs. These are the variety you
will need, but in spite of them you will still spend quite a
time playing hunt-the-pillowcase with the children. Unless
you are prepared to wear a scarf or an old knitted hat all
day long, you will also find out why most coastal-dwelling
people have short hair. The best thing to do is just accept
it and buy a long hair piece for those odd occasions when
you have the strength left to go out to dinner. It's just the
price you pay for that beautiful view.

On a personal note, if you have children it is absolute-ly essential that you have some foolproof way of getting clothes dry as they will probably come in at least three times a day requiring a total change of outfit, having fallen in the stream, the sea, or just been a couple of miles from the house when the heaven's have opened. Those marvellous all-in-one waterproof suits are perfect for the little ones, but they only seem to make them for small children and after that you are on your own. A tumble-drier is not the answer. Back in 'civilisation' you may have had a reliable source of electricity, but out here it is quite liable to go off at least once a week, for an indeterminate period of time. Then, of course, it also goes off every time the wind is above force seven or there is a clap of thunder in the far distance. How the lightening always manages to strike our electricity pylon without fail is something beyond my understanding, but a good ear for the weather forecast is an absolute must so that you can make preparation in time before being plunged into darkness.

Electricity, like sex, is one of the things you don't re-alise how much you miss until you do without it for any period of time. So buy yourself a good supply of candles and a few of those lovely old paraffin lamps. These will supply the light, but will not supply the heat to dry all those damp clothes. If you can't buy one, then make one of those marvellous pull up and down wooden frames that hang on the ceiling by the fireplace for the smaller more vital bits and pieces. The larger objects can always go out-side on the line and you can hope the rain will pause long enough for the wind to dry them. You will soon get quite adept at estimating if the blowing wind is stronger than the driving rain and will in fact manage to dry out your clothes to the extent that they can be hung over the backs of chairs for a final airing. Your house may have all the appearances of a Chinese laundry, but so will everybody else's, so not to worry!

One of the great things about living in remote areas, is that all worries you may have once had about 'outward appearances' soon disappear forever. People are sure to come to call just as you have spread the clothes all over the place or the children have just let the goat into the kitchen because they felt sorry for it getting wet outside. It came as a great relief to me to find that everyone else lived in the chaos that we did and that everyone else's children were quite definitely grubby by lunch-time and only clean for about thirty minutes each day, just after being slung in the bath after tea. After all, you are going to find out that there are many more important things than washing the clothes and the children all day long for the sake of appearances. The same law applies to housework. If you have the time or the energy to do it, then fine. If not, don't worry about it – nobody else will. You, like everybody else, will come to value people for what they are, not for the cleanliness of their houses or their children.

Finding that we couldn't buy a car as we didn't qualify for the HP not being house-owners, we leased one instead and suddenly we were mobile again. This was probably a good thing as it began to rain steadily that autumn and didn't really stop for a year and a half. Pat chopped great piles of logs for me before he left each time as he had reached the inevitable conclusion that no amount of practice was going to improve my wood-cutting abilities. We also decided to make a vegetable garden ready for the spring. If there wasn't any soil we would just have to bring soil in, so we got to work building a small low wall round the prospective plot to try and stop any erosion that might occur. Then sack after sack of leaf mould was lugged from the nearby woods until it all began to look just ready for planting in the spring. All this being done in the pouring rain.

Small, frothy streams began to chatter and burble their way down through the garden en route to the sea and as

each grey dawn followed another, these became noisier and faster and began to join together until there was a roaring, tumbling waterfall just outside the back door. We dug frantic troughs to take the water away from the house and listened in vain each night for some reduction in the roar of the water. Luckily it was during a time when Pat was at home that one night we awoke to hear Markie calling to us from his staircase. He was saying something to the effect that he couldn't get downstairs to the loo because Pepper had spent a big penny on the floor. Not being at my best at 3.00am, it took a while for me to stagger downstairs to see what was the matter and about three steps from the bottom, my lower half came into quite definite contact with about two feet of water. Not still, calm water, but a rushing, raging torrent coming from the direction of the kitchen and disappearing in the general direction of the front door. Definitely nothing to do with the dogs who had jumped up onto the draining board in the kitchen to avoid the rising water. There wasn't time to give way to hysterics as Pat set me to work to rescue anything electrical that came to hand and place it well above water level. Things were relieved a bit when he opened the front door which gave the water a more definite way out, added to which now the rain and wind blew in. We couldn't actually get out through the back door due to the sheer force of the water hammering upon it, but on creeping round the side of the house to investigate, it looked in the torch-light a bit like Niagara Falls with our house about halfway down. We rescued what we could, but afraid to turn on any lights and wet through, we took the most sensible option and went back upstairs to bed.

In the morning the rain had stopped, the waterfall gone back to its size of twenty-four hours beforehand and most of the water in the house had drained away too, leaving the odd puddle on the floor, just like the ones we had seen on that first visit to the house. But anything that had been on the ground, or sitting up to two feet above the ground, was soaking wet. This included such things as the armchairs and the carpet. We only had two carpets, so it was decided to try and dry them first. The one in the dining-room just fell into a million pieces when we moved it. Obviously a write-off, but the one in the living-room was rolled up by Pat and hauled outside by the entire family. It's quite amazing how heavy a wet carpet is. All our attempts to get it up and over the washing line to dry failed. That was until Pat had the idea of putting the carpet over the line on the ground, then hitching the line up over a tree branch and then down again to the tow bar on the car. All he had to do then was drive carefully forwards and the carpet rose into the air. Using the car as an anchor, he tied a few of those intricate knots sailors use and the job was done. The whole thing would have been perfect if it hadn't rained again, so it was nearly three weeks before an attempt could be made to get it back down after Pat had gone back to work. On inspecting the knots it became obvious that the rain and the weight had done their work and there was no way they were going to come undone. The only option was to cut the rope and thus the carpet fell back down into the mud. Working on the principle that the mud would dry inside and could be hoovered up, the children and I somehow lugged it back into the living-room and got it back down. It was never quite the same again.

The second flood wasn't quite so bad in that the water only rose about a foot high and, in anticipation, Pat had rolled up the carpet and balanced it on top of the sofa the night before, but by the time the third one came my sanity was in serious doubt. This occurred while Pat was away and during the late afternoon. There had been a violent storm all day long and we had been keeping an eye on the rapidly increasing waterfall all day. Anticipating the worst, somehow between us we got the carpet up, balanced the chairs on top of each other and generally made ready for the next flood. Whilst attempting to feed the children tea in an effort to remain calm and unflustered, it began to register with a certain sort of detached fascination how water was starting to come up through cracks in the concrete floors. By the time tea had finished there was just time to put the two smallest children upstairs on dry land and for Jason and me to start brushing the rising water out of the front door. It was a bit like King Canute trying to hold back the tide and had about the same effect. Suddenly, out of the storm appeared a neighbour and his wife who had come to ask me to help them! It seemed that as he was a fisherman he was worried about the state of his boat down at the pier. Their car, being a bit ancient, could not get through the flood waters covering the roads on the way there. As we had a relatively new car they wondered if I would be good enough to drive him down to the pier to have a look at it, while his wife looked after my children and did her best to keep the flood waters at bay in our house. Lending him one of Pat's North Sea survival suits like the one already covering me, and although at one point water was coming through the car doors, we eventually made it down to the pub and the pier. It's difficult to recall the exact reason which caused me to then get out of the car, probably just following him, but it was my first experience of the full blast of an Atlantic storm in winter. The sleet was coming across the pier horizontally, making it impossible to see anything and cutting and lashing into my face. Although my body was protected by the survival suit, it was impossible to stand against the wind. Forced down onto my hands and knees, my body strained against the elements, we crawled up the seaweed-covered pier towards his rapidly filling boat. About half-way there the thought struck me – what the hell was I doing? Even if I made it to the boat, I could be of no possible help. No way was I going to go aboard and start bailing. I was no sailor and even on the calmest of days, I was more likely to be in the way than of any use. So with these thoughts in my mind and hoping he would understand I crawled back to the car. It was necessary to make four more journeys down to the pier during the night to help him check and bail the boat with the result that his was the only boat that didn't sink. In between times we passed the long hours bailing out my house and laughing at it all over cups of tea. They say that a problem shared is a problem solved and it certainly was true in this case.

Meanwhile that spring and summer, the rain continued and never really let up for longer than a day or two. 'Soft' the locals called it, while 'bloody damp' was considerably nearer the mark. On the practical side it meant that every day we faced the problem of keeping ourselves, our clothes and the house bearably dry. For all its olde-worlde charm, the main fireplace was a disaster area. Unable to either chop or afford enough wood for its formidable appetite, we certainly were not getting as much heat pro rata as effort put in. Something had to be done and done quickly. Now, it had come to our notice when visiting several friends in the area whose cottages were always warm and snug, that the source of this heat was usually a range of some description. They provided not only heat, but sometimes hot water and you could also cook on them and not be dependant on the intermittent electricity. It seemed the perfect answer, so we set off to town.

If you are at all prone to the odd heart attack, it is worth considering staying at home because you will find the cost of a new range (of the variety that does all those marvellous things) somewhat prohibitive, but if you then make further enquiries, you will also find that second-hand ones can be had. It is always prudent to bear in mind that ranges have probably been around since the Iron Age and so the term 'second-hand' can mean that it has been in one family for several generations. It therefore will have become a cherished family member during this time and the fact that it is now out in the field or dumped by the side of the road with grass growing in it, will in no way diminish its price down from the exorbitant to the ridiculous. However, if you persevere, you will probably find one near enough to your limited funds.

If you think you are mad to buy something that has been lying outside for the last twenty years, just wait till you try and pick it up! Ranges are made of very heavy metal and require either a team of brawny men or a tractor to move them from a to b. If you organise a tractor, you will still need the team of men to get it from b into the house. Having done this, and subsequently reattached all the bits that have dropped off en route, you must then seal the chimney with another suitably heat-proof piece of metal, having first remembered to cut a hole for the range chimney to go through. We were all quite impressed with the job Pat made of it and tried desperately hard not to be too discouraged when, after lighting it, smoke poured from every joint, crack and opening. You will remember at this point that he had sealed the chimney, so we found it quite hard to accept his reassurances from our vantage point out in the road that it would cease smoking as it got hotter. But eventually it calmed down and when the air got to breathable level, we went back in again to start living with it.

A range is a bit like a flower in some ways in that it seems to function better if you talk nicely to it. It takes about six months to learn to live with it and get used to all its strange little ways, but eventually you will appreciate its needs and demands and it will become another thing that you cannot live without. It certainly made a world of difference to our cottage – from being damp and draughty to cosy and warm. Learning to cook on it was a longer process. You can bet that if the range has been boiling hot all day, the minute you place something in the oven, it will go out. Again, like a flower, you need to nurture it gently. Kicking it will only damage your foot. But slowly, a whole new approach to cooking will open up. All those marvellous old recipes remembered from your dim, distant childhood will reappear, and such things as stews and casseroles and steamed puddings – all of which you had long ceased to make because they used up far too much electricity – will become part of your daily fare. Nothing tastes quite the same as a roast cooked in a range or nothing smells like crusty brown loaves of bread just emerging from its oven. Mind you, this doesn't always combine well with the smell of drying welly boots that are hung over the top; but it's a safe bet to say that once you and your range have learned to live with each other, you will be its willing slave for life.

However, we had to face the fact that it was not possible to carry on with just surviving all these floods. Something had to be done. After considering all the options, it was decided to put in storm drains of a suitably large size under the house from the back to the front. Then the waterfall could come down, go straight into the storm drain, under the house and out the other side of the road. This did mean

digging up all the concrete floors to install the drains, but it was to solve the problem for us permanently. One interesting fact did emerge, however, during the digging up of the floors. Old drains were found running roughly in the same direction. These had just been made of stones propped up against each other forming a tunnel, which had long since collapsed. These tunnels bore evidence of having been occupied by otters and they were what was probably responsible for the 'ghost' noises that had so terrified our predecessors. The otters had most likely used the tunnels for a quick, safe way up the mountain and when a collapse occurred, they must have scraped and scratched at the rocks trying to claw a way through, hence making the noises in the night!

Anyway, we put any lingering fears we might have about ghosts down to this and would have continued quite happily if it hadn't been for Jason coming home from the beach one day, quite hysterical. He said he had seen a man coming down towards him all dressed in black and with no face! We calmed him down, saying it must have been a diver or a seal, but we never really could convince him. But living in a land so rich in legends and lore, leprechauns, pots of gold and rainbows, these fairy folk sometimes seem to be just half a dream away and life is such that you are never quite sure on which side of that dream you will waken.

4

LIVING WITHOUT IT

Our first relatively dry and cosy winter came as a great relief to us all, and then as suddenly as it had started, the rain stopped. For six weeks right through Easter the sun shone. It was warm enough to spend lazy days down at the beach, though the children required energetic games of football after swimming to start the circulation going again. In March the sunshine, which had been slowly creeping up the fields a little nearer to the cottage each day, eventually reached the front of the house and flooded in through the windows. After six winter months of shade and gloom and staring enviously at the odd sunny day on the other side of the bay, a multitude of very necessary spring-cleaning jobs were revealed in its golden radiance. So it was out with the paintbrush, down with the curtains, off with the sheets and away with the cobwebs.

The washing machine, which had endured through the birth and early life of both boys, been put into storage for months, moved from one country to another, flooded twice and subjected to all kinds of damp, made gorse and rocks. Jason was able to follow the exact route of the pipe, whilst Markie accompanied me carrying the bag with the tools and Gemma slept peacefully in the baby carrier on my back. Further and further up we climbed, getting hotter and hotter, but still Jason reported no sign of a break, until eventually all four of us stood together at the point where the pipe entered the pool. The pipe was fine and intact; it was just the water that was missing. The little spring that normally trickled out through the rocks to fill our only water source had dried up and gone, leaving a lot of cracked mud, some dead pond weed and no doubt, a few cross frogs.

Back down at the house again, the children were questioned closely. Surely they must have seen some other stream or spring in their explorations of the mountainside. a half-hearted attempt at Gemma's nappies and then died right in the middle of my spring-cleaning epic. Taking the top off and peering inside revealed a whole load of very complicated wiring, a lot of rust and no easy answer. There was nothing left to do but to screw the top back on, leave it until Pat's return and resort to doing all the washing by hand. With two of my children still in nappies, plus all the dirty washing created by the spring-cleaning, it very soon became obvious why somebody had invented the washing machine. If they hadn't already done it, by the end of a week I would have invented it for them. Slaving away with boiling saucepans on the range and the bath constantly full of soaking washing brings home the full realisation of how much one depends on certain household items. However this was absolutely nothing compared to the events which were about to to unfold, because after about three weeks and just before Pat came back, the water stopped again.

Setting off up the mountain complete with every tool we could possibly need to mend breaks in pipes or extract frogs from same, the sun beat warmly down on our backs and made me feel almost cheerful scrambling upwards through

But there were none. How was it possible to be so awash with water one minute and totally without it the next? Meanwhile at the bottom of the fields, the sea sparkled and shone in the most maddening fashion and the sun continued to blaze away without even the smallest semblance of a rain cloud on the horizon. Pat's return soon after was no help. All it did was to increase the amount of dirty washing piling up everywhere. We resorted to disposable nappies for the little ones and Pat accompanied by Jason drove repeatedly down the four miles to the nearest spring well with every available container. From making local enquiries we gathered that this was no one-off occurrence and most of the spring wells had a habit of going dry during a long fine spell. Unless you actually went to the expense and trouble of drilling for water or had a nearby reliable stream or river, this was just one of life's little hazards not mentioned in the self-sufficiency books which always assume that you will have a surplus of natural supplies immediately to hand.

The children, who with great delight had thought that this would mean they wouldn't have to wash any more, were somewhat surprised to be route marched down to the sea each morning and immersed in the icy water. I was desperate for a bath myself, but somehow the thought of a brisk swim in April in the Atlantic, no matter how warm the sun felt, was out of the question. Even Pat saying that he thought he had fixed the washing machine (though he couldn't test it until he had water again) did nothing to lift my spirits. There was nothing for it but to get on with as many jobs as possible and just enjoy the sunshine. On the plus side, we did all get the most marvellous suntans, which resulted as much from the dirt as from the heat, whilst dreaming of all the rainy days to come.

Living without water was an unexpected hazard of self-sufficiency but it could be endured, as could the lapses in the electricity supply, because we could reassure ourselves that the loss was only temporary. My other fears and phobias of a more permanent nature had to be faced differently. Coming from the UK where one could nip into the Health Centre for every little snuffle, the idea of living sixteen miles from the nearest doctor, let alone eighty miles from the nearest large hospital, was initially my main worry. It wasn't terribly reassuring when, eventually getting round to visiting a doctor to confirm my pregnancy after our arrival, I had my hand held and arm patted comfortingly and was told that I would know soon enough myself. Maybe this was an Irish ante-natal examination? I couldn't be sure, but it seemed all he was prepared to do. However, the doctor soon dropped my arm when we made enquiries as to the possibility of having the baby at home. The horror he displayed was something akin to being told we planned to poison the child at birth. It was out of the question, he gasped. All mothers have their babies in Cork he informed me and that was that. No amount of trying to point out that Mark had arrived on this planet in twenty minutes flat and how the hell would we get the eighty miles to the hospital in that time would budge him. But despite Pat buying a special do-it-yourself home birth's book, Gemma did make her arrival in Cork after all. They just induced me when I went up for my final ante-natal about a week before she was due, with no fuss at all. And it still comes as a source of wonder to me that practically without exception, all babies from around here manage to be born in Cork.

Once you have staggered out in the middle of the night with your sick child a few times and driven pell-mell the sixteen miles to the doctor, only to find that the patient is fast asleep with all symptoms seemingly vanished by the time you get there, you will begin to settle down a little and start to throw a modicum of common sense into the pot. Doctors appear to have a second sense on the telephone as to whether the patient is really at death's door or not, and eventually, given a little time, you will acquire this too. It is in this way that the doctors manage to cover the large, remote areas of their practices out here. All minor illnesses are coped with at home and you only bother the doctor if you really believe something is wrong.

Into this category come broken bones. If you have small children, especially small boys, they will almost certainly break bits of themselves despite any precautions you may care to take. Repeatedly warning them of the consequences of jumping off the top of a five-bar gate will have absolutely no effect, until eventually the inevitable will happen. It was probably hearing the screams and seeing Mark rushing inside waving his arm frantically, with the bit from six inches above his wrist flapping up and down independently of the rest, that caused me to faint on the spot and be of absolutely no help to anyone. Luckily Pat was home and able to dump me in a chair with my head between my knees, whilst he made full use of the first-aid training learned on his oil-rig and expertly strapped Markie up. By the time my head cleared enough to stand up again, they had all gone off to the hospital, with Jason giving Pat the help he needed. Not only was I mortified by my reaction to this crisis; it worried me even more what would happen in the same situation if Pat had not been there. However, several broken bones later, he reassured me that if you have to cope in an emergency, you do.

The beautiful hot weather of that spring had wrought a few changes in me too. There's nothing quite like tentatively trying on an old bikini to bring about an instant crash diet. After three children and being cloistered inside for over a year due to the weather, combined with an excess of steamed treacle puddings, something would definitely have to be done. As it was obviously going to cause me great pain and suffering to refrain from all the fattening goodies, it seemed reasonable to go the whole hog and give up smoking at the same time. If you're going to be miserable, you might as well be really and truly and rottenly miserable and get the whole thing over at once. By the end of the first week of my enforced regime, the children were learning quickly to keep out of my way and be sweet and nice to me at all times and they passed this survival information on to Pat when he returned.

That was when the headaches started to get worse. Originally plagued with just the odd severe head pains over the past year, as the diet and non-smoking routine continued into its third month, so the duration and intensity of the pain increased. 'Totally psychosomatic' Pat reassured me, though he did take the precaution of sending me to a specialist in Cork who diagnosed migraine. The specialist also said that if we could find out what had triggered off the sequence of migraine, we could possibly cure it and in the same breath wrote off any idea that it could be the diet or the lack of cigarettes. Tackling the problem like Sherlock Holmes, we slowly eliminated one possible cause after another until there was only one left. The range. As our bed was directly above it and there was nowhere else in the room it could go, we would have to change bedrooms with the children. Whether it was just the chaos of the all-change, or the move away from whatever fumes leaked from the old range, it cured me good and proper and being sick for so long had done wonders for my diet and cravings for a cigarette. To this day I've never had another one, though I can't quite say the same for the treacle puds.

What is absolutely essential in remote areas such as these is the necessity of having good, reliable neighbours: The sort of people you can ring up at 7.30am, announce you are bringing two of your children over immediately, give no reason and they do not ask. The most important thing to realise about good neighbours is that you have to be one too. In other words, it is reciprocal. If you can't give as much as you can take, then life away-from-it-all is not for you. Whether or not you have children yourself, people don't foist theirs on you without a very good reason. This is especially true in Ireland where children are accepted everywhere without question. They are as much a familiar sight in the pubs as in the restaurants and cafes. If you go out to supper with people, it is automatically accepted that you will bring the children with you. This has the practical advantage of eliminating the need for babysitters on all but a few occasions. So when you are asked, you presume it important and the reason why can always wait till it is proffered later.

One small setback in an area as remote as this, is that if you have to make the journey to the hospital, it's quite possible you could be away for anything up to two or three days, so babysitting can sometimes be a somewhat extended affair. After a severe bout of whooping cough, it became more and more apparent that Gemma couldn't hear properly, and as she couldn't hear and hadn't learned to talk yet, she screamed instead. Eventually, when nobody could stand it any longer, we took her to the doctor. Several doctors and several weeks later she was in hospital having an operation on both ears for deafness, which thankfully was completely successful. During these repeated trips to

Cork the other two children had to be farmed out on numerous occasions and often they weren't at the same house where they started out from on my return – the whole neighbourhood had just coped in my absence with animals, children and all.

During my initial period of being a grass widow, the novelty of having to cope with absolutely everything on my own kept me fully occupied. The thing that bothered me most was my totally irrational fear of heights which had only become apparent on our arrival in Ireland. It may have had something to do with the sheep that sleep in the middle of the road here and refuse to move when one encounters them on an early morning outing. Trying to negotiate the car around a sleeping sheep with a mountain on one side and a sheer, unfenced drop on the other is a little hazardous to say the least. So is the probability of rounding any corner and coming face to face with a herd of cows standing chewing the cud in the middle of the road, or being taken to market, driven somewhat erratically by a load of children and several barking dogs. There are also those suicidal sheepdogs that lurk in the bushes and rush out snapping at your tyres as you pass by. The gut reaction of an animal lover such as myself was to immediately swerve to miss them. Having actually killed two such dogs within a few months of arriving, it was pointed out to me that you should just drive straight on ignoring them. The dogs don't expect anybody to actually be stupid enough to try and miss them and are completely caught unawares if you attempt to do so. There's probably some logic in this, if you look deep enough, and so surely there should be some logical way of solving my new found fear of heights?

Facing up to irrational fears boldly was the way one book suggested, so next time Pat was home he was a little taken aback to be asked to take me up the nearest mountain. In all truth it wasn't really a mountain as its total height was only just over a thousand feet, but it looked big enough to me from the bottom. Going up really wasn't too bad as long as my eyes were glued to the solid face of the mountain in front of me and didn't look down. It was arriving at the top that caused the problem. Restraining the terrible overwhelming urge to throw myself forward over the edge was one thing, but the way the whole landscape seemed to sway giddily up and down was another. Half an hour lying with my head under a gorse bush and clasping a rock firmly in both hands got me to the stage where the downhill journey could be attempted, but it soon became quite obvious that any descent would have to be done backwards. If you stand forwards you can see where you are going and the terrible drop before you get there. Backwards is just like coming up, but in reverse. It also takes a great deal longer and it didn't cure me at all in any way. The solution turned out to be having three children with the sure-footedness and steady eyes of mountain goats and making them do all the high-up jobs instead. This is called compromise and compromise is something you will learn to do very quickly if you want to survive.

It became necessary to compromise on one fact of being a grass widow, and that was the attitude that because Pat was away I should remain at home in a sort of enforced personal purdah. Of course, taking the children with me as chaperones was sort of OK, but the thought of either going out on my own, or God Forbid with another man, was akin to adultery. Being fairly strong-minded and finding the lack of adult company (male or female) somewhat unstimulating, turning down an invitation was out of the question. The only method to stop wagging tongues was to go out openly and take no notice of the odd horrified look coming my way, though it was hard to repress a grin when, if it was necessary to bring me a message, the men would either send their wives with it, or if forced to bring it themselves, never set foot across the threshold just in case they might get raped or something equally dire.

In retrospect, what was also amusing about the way they regarded me, was the way the local lunatics were treated. Now any community has its share of local drunks, colourful characters and those slightly touched by the rising of the full moon. Whilst in the city they would be ignored and shunned, here in the country they are tolerated almost to the point of acceptance. Whilst one can fully appreciate the humane points of this attitude, there are those that take full advantage of it and consequently can get away with practically anything they choose to do.

This was brought home vividly to us when it was just getting dark one evening in early April and the little children had just been persuaded to go to bed. The thought of a nice peaceful evening by myself took a bit of a nosedive when one of the locals, more than a little affected by both a drop of the hard stuff and the full moon, decided to set fire to the entire peninsula. Somewhat akin to Nero, but without the fiddle, he obviously intended to get a big kick out of watching it burn. The fact that there were houses along this peninsula (including ours) didn't deter him for a minute and he happily walked along the mountainside setting fires as he went. Now, gorse is very inflammable, especially after a long dry spell and when I happened to wander into the kitchen to get myself a cup of coffee and found myself confronted by the sight of fifty-foot high flames outside the window, it was cause for great alarm. Whipped by the wind and accompanied by a loud roaring, the fire rushed towards our cottage at a terrifying speed. Recovering my wits, the children were hauled out of bed and deposited in the middle of the road, dogs and cats evicted whilst the fire-brigade in Kenmare was phoned for immediate assistance.

Knowing it was only a voluntary brigade and that precious time would pass before they could assemble and drive out the sixteen miles, it was obviously essential not to panic. Jason was stationed in the road by the animal shed, ready to release them when the oncoming flames reached a certain point, whilst the two little ones leaped up and down in the road overjoyed with all the marvellous excitement. It was left to me to rush in and out of the house trying desperately to think of what was most important to save. It's worth wondering why, at times like this, it's either an old armchair or a four-drawer metal filing cabinet that seems to be the most important thing worth rescuing? Logic kept telling me that Pat, on his return, wouldn't be too pleased to find that he had no possessions except all his old bills and letters and would want to know why his fishing rods hadn't been the first things to be thrown out. The result was that nothing much got evicted except ourselves. Presuming it to be a gorse fire that had accidentally got out of control, the sheer speed and noise of its approach was terrifying. Then just as all seemed lost, shortly before the fire reached the animal shed the wind changed direction slightly and the fire roared up and behind the cottage and on down the peninsula.

Fifteen minutes later the local fire brigade arrived. Enthusiastic and dedicated as they were, the welcome sight was somewhat dampened by the fact that they didn't actually have any water, there being no mains water hereabouts, our water pipe being somewhere up in the middle of the blazing inferno, and the sea a bit too far off to rush up and down with buckets. But they set about the bits still burning with shovels, went off to warn anybody else who was in the path of the fire and didn't let the fact that they had a waterless fire engine deter them one bit. Although they were to remain for several more hours, there really was nothing they could do except let the fire burn itself out. The slight change of wind direction meant that the human habitation was saved, but the mountainside was devastated. Thousands of yards of fencing, water pipes, wild animal life, spring flowers and anything else in its path was totally eliminated

and the sheer extent of this madman's spree only became evident the following morning.

Having spent the night sleeping in fits and starts in case the wind should start the fire up again near the house, when Jason went to check on our water pipe all that remained was a trail of blackened plastic on the ground. The most horrifying thing of all was that from the places where the fires had been started, the arsonist would have had a clear view of our cottage and know full well that we were inside it. The local view of him being 'that poor man' was something impossible for me to come to terms with, and so was the notion that idiots like this should be allowed to remain to roam as free as air and as mad as hatters.

After being in a place for a few years, it gets hard to remember that you are incomers and not locals, especially in view of the friendship and general welcome, and although you may have strong views on certain matters, they may not necessarily be the view of the community as a whole. The fact that I actually enjoyed having periods of time apart from my husband and didn't make any secret of it was regarded with a great deal of suspicion. For me it was a chance to 'do my own thing' unfettered by having to conform to the demands of society or the accepted view of being a 'wife'. Having to be both Dad and Mum to my children proved to be fun and brought us all much closer together as friends than we had ever been. A bit of imposed abstinence does wonders for your sex life and although sometimes a month away seemed like forever, the knowledge that it was to be followed by a month at home made it doubly worthwhile. However, old customs die hard in country areas and going into someone's home and finding the women waiting on table whilst the men and boys ate first was quite a shock initially, as was finding quite so many things labelled as 'women's work'.

It was also hard to come to terms with the fact that the word 'punctuality' doesn't exist here. If a person says they will do something, then they will do it. When they do it is another matter. Only the passing of time will help you to accept this and to realise that it isn't the time when the job is done that is important, it's the doing of it well. There is a definite general feeling that Fate will take care of those who err. One way or another bad deeds have a way of catching up with you without any outside interference. It's just all a matter of time. More importantly, living without many of the accepted conveniences of our previous life had taught us all to come to terms with any fears and phobias we might have and to bring it home to us that there is more than one way of skinning a cat.

5

BIRDS OF A FEATHER

Having taken nearly a year to reach the stage where we were warm and comfortable within, it was a little disheartening to look without. Nearly a year had swept by since the self-sufficiency book had last been opened, which meant that things were not exactly going to plan and it was certainly time to pull our socks up and put things to rights. An examination of the vegetable garden was not encouraging as it was no longer there. Not even the stone walls remained. The winter floods had made short work of them and the ground was back to being just two inches of packed mud over bedrock. The vegetable garden was to be rebuilt many times, resorting to such extremes as posts sunk in concrete, but none was very successful. The nearest we came to ever getting from the seed to the crop was when we resorted to Grow Bags, but these were expensive and the home-made kind found it hard to stay together for a whole season. The decision was made that the most practical thing to do was to abandon the idea of crops, with the exception of a few hardy herbs, and practise

our self-sufficiency on livestock instead. So we went back
to the bible for the answer.

Hens were the obvious choice. We had a shed (of
sorts), and thirty-six acres for them to 'free range' on.
Pat was put to work on roofing the small shed and then
building nesting boxes and perches, whilst my job was to
go to the monthly fair in Kenmare and purchase six brown,
clucking, point-of-lay pullets and a large sack of something
called layer's mash. They were then introduced to their
new home, brought bowls of steaming mash each morning,
whilst we sat back and waited for the eggs. Whatever else
'point of lay' might have meant, it definitely didn't have
anything to do with laying eggs, because two months later,
we were still waiting. They certainly looked happy enough
scratching away and murmuring to themselves all the while.
Even such devious measures as buying half a dozen shop
eggs and putting them in the nesting boxes hoping to trick
them into thinking one of the others had beaten them to
it, didn't work. It was all in vain.

On taking recourse to the self-sufficiency book once
more, and reading right to the end this time, we found it
said that feeding your hens too much will stop them laying.
An instant diet ensued, at which point all their feathers
started to drop out. Relating this to the diet, when in fact
it just happened to be the start of the autumn moult (and
when hens moult, they don't lay anyway), it was definitely
a no-win situation. Pat didn't think my idea of getting a
cockerel for them would make any difference, and as far
as egg-laying went, it didn't. However, the cockerel did
look pretty rounding up all the hens and marching them
wherever he wanted to go in orderly ranks, though he drove
us all scatty at 5.00am every morning with his crowing.

It also said in the book that if you want your hens to lay
early in the year, they must be well fed over the winter. By
spring numerous sacks of layer's mash had been consumed
by our feathered friends' – even the left-overs were boiled up

twice a day from a saucepan which emitted the most ghastly smell. Everybody was instructed that they must always try and be nice to them (if necessary between clenched teeth), but I think it was the effect of my going out one day and threatening them all with the cooking pot that brought about a mass laying session. Eggs at last. Now, it won't take long for you to discover that if your hens lay six eggs every day of the week, not only will you have forty-two eggs a week, but a general revolt on your hands from the family who will have got fed up with having eggs twice a day. You can either buy an old-fashioned cookery book like Mrs Beeton's which puts about three dozen eggs in each recipe, or sell some. The latter is preferable as you will need something to refill the coffers after having spent so much on layer's mash.

Just when you have sold them all and have got a nice round of regular customers, the hens will go broody. You can tell when this takes place as they get all puffed up and attack you on sight to prevent you removing the eggs from the nesting box. So it's back to no eggs again, but there is nothing quite so enchanting as your first baby chick. When you have got about thirty-five baby chickens, the prospect of how you are going to feed them all will rear its ugly head. Thirty-five babies, six mothers and a cockerel at the end of one year is a daunting problem, especially in view of the fact that you could end up with several hundred by the next year. As the ones you have now will have scratched up any bits of grass attempting to grow and their droppings will be absolutely everywhere, the thought of the havoc and damage that can be wrought by a further thirty-five will make the idea of roast chicken seem positively wonderful.

In order to get the chicken from the nest to the table, you have got to kill it. When two unexpected visitors arrived for lunch one day, it was a case of having plenty of spare cockerels and no excuses left. Pat read the page on 'Killing and Preparing a Chicken' and marched forth with a purposeful look on his face, followed by all three children. He enticed the cockerels over with some food, picked up the first one, strangled it and threw it down in the corner. This process was then repeated with a second and a third. Having been considerably impressed by this expertise, it came as a bit of a shock when the second one got up from the pile of corpses and went back to the food and started eating again. Definitely just nervous reaction, said Pat as we all stood around watching the cockerel, waiting for it to keel over. Ten minutes later he had to admit that perhaps he hadn't done it quite right, but no amount of chasing and running could persuade that cockerel to be caught again. The other two were eaten and by that evening everybody felt sorry for Number Two and decided to leave him alone. He was to last another three years before eventually becoming dinner for a passing fox, but ever since that day, instead of crowing he barked like a dog – Pat had broken his voice box, not his neck!

Encouraged by our tenuous success with the chickens, it seemed to be a natural progression to get some ducks and four teenage ducks were duly purchased. The self-sufficiency book stated clearly that ducks and hens didn't like living together, so alterations had to be made to the shed, in order that they could have separate living quarters. As these have to be both fox and rat proof, you will spend quite a time wrestling with chicken wire and nails – not easy in a confined space. Then there was the question of water. Now whilst there was more than enough water passing through the place the majority of the time, there was not a pond or a regular stream on the mountain side, so Pat set to work until he had created a nice deep hole. Then, on a day when the heavens opened sufficiently, he got hold of his pickaxe and diverted several of the many rushing streams down into it. As the pond was lined with black plastic sheeting, it didn't take long to fill and the ducks were obviously delighted with it. So were the children who had to be discouraged from spending most of the day splashing around and thus terrorising the ducks. These grew from being teenagers into three lady ducks and one handsome drake. Even better, they obviously had an absolute passion for a meal of giant Kerry slugs and before long had quite effectively reduced their numbers. It still wasn't possible to plant anything, because now the chickens would scratch it all up again, but all the same it was a nice thought.

When the ducks were not eating slugs, they quite happily beat up the chickens and ate all their layer's mash and, on their improved diet, it wasn't long before they started laying eggs too. Unlike chickens, ducks are not at all fussy about which nest they lay their eggs in, and even when the first one went broody, the others all insisted on squashing in with it and laying their eggs in with the ones she was sitting on. To avoid much confusion we tried marking the eggs, but this meant that each morning you had to battle with an irate mummy duck to remove the surplus eggs, none of which she wanted you to have. Then to top it all, when the second and third duck went broody as well, they all tried to sit on top of the same eggs. Putting other eggs into other nests was of no attraction at all, and only by getting some old fish barrels, putting some hay and a selection of eggs into each one and then barricading the respective mummy duck inside it, was order restored. After a few days of imprisonment, they were content to keep to their own fish barrel and when the four weeks of incubation were over, we were presented with three batches of quite adorable fluffy ducklings.

At this point you will discover why the self-sufficiency book say that ducks make rotten mothers and to use a broody hen if at all possible. For starters, it is quite likely that one of the mummy ducks will sneak out at night and entice ducklings from the other nests into hers, so that she

ends up each morning with a whole load of very confused babies. She will beat off the other mothers in no uncertain fashion and after a couple of days of this, they will get disheartened and wander off after the drake, showing no particular concern at their sudden loss. Our aggressive mummy duck sat defiantly with her enlarged family until it became obvious that she had no-one to quarrel with any more, so she set off in search of them, dragging all the little ones behind her in a long procession. Now, if you are about two inches high and have webbed feet, mountaineering through grass and flowers and rocks all much taller than you can be a daunting prospect and it wasn't long before some got left behind. If these didn't die from exhaustion, they were quickly picked off by the big, black crows that had hung around the apple trees since the birth. One rescue attempt after another was made, but slowly the numbers of the babies dwindled until only the two strongest survived to adulthood. Both of these proved to be drakes.

The following spring saw us determined not to have a

repeat of the previous year. Still unable to provide a broody hen as mother, because the ducks went broody many weeks before the hens, the minute the little ducklings hatched, they were whisked away from the mothers and put into a separate cosy cage complete with food and water. Unbeknown to us, when baby ducklings shelter under their mothers during the first days of life, they get from her feathers the special waterproofing that keeps them dry and afloat in water. Without the mother duck, they still have the instinct to get into the nearest water, but they drown. There is nothing quite so galling as hindsight. Although the baby ducks produce their own waterproofing within a few days, until they are about a week old, you must keep them away from anything but the very shallowest water. Once they reached about six weeks old, we decided to let the survivors out for the odd graze or two on the young spring grass. Without a mother, although practically fully grown, the young ducks huddled together in groups, making an easy target for the wretched crows once again. We rushed to the rescue, but despite our best efforts only two drakes and one duck survived. There is really only one answer to the problem of rearing baby ducks and that is to keep them confined in a cage, with the mother duck, until they are least ten weeks old: that way you can be certain of success. Although Pat had always been an ardent fan of roast duck, none of us could bring ourselves to contemplate eating the survivors of all these massacres and so it was decided to take the young drakes and set them free on the nearest river where at least they would have a fighting chance of reaching adulthood.

Once we had everything set up for the ducks, it seemed only natural to throw in a few geese as well. Having negotiated with a local farmer the purchase of the young geese he had reared that year, we were a bit alarmed when he insisted we take the parents as well. Although this was somewhat in excess of what we had anticipated paying, it was a question of all or none, and so six geese ended up coming home with us. Before leaving we took the precaution of asking which were male and which were female as they all looked exactly the same to us. This was greeted with the usual nudge and a wink and being told to wait till spring time for the proof. It wasn't necessary to wait quite such a long time to find out which was the dominant adult male, as it repeatedly attacked us all as soon as we released them. As the young ones were nearly the same size as the two adults, any further enquiry into their gender would have to wait until they had settled in a bit.

The self-sufficiency book said that geese lived mainly on grass (and we had plenty of that), and that they mated for life. A little perturbed that brother and sister would mate for life come spring, we decided to try and tell which was a male and swop it with another goose breeder for an unrelated one. But they all seemed as aggressive as each other, flying across the field at us in a flurry of outstretched heads and wings. Although the book said that the females held their heads and necks in a different way from the males, this obviously requires an experienced eye. In the end, we just picked the one who attacked us most frequently and swopped him for another which we were assured was a male. Now geese might mate for life, but they also form family units for life and are not at all happy with brother substitutions. Despite his efforts to be friendly, the others harassed him from morning till night and it was over a year before they would even let him sleep in the same place as them. Come spring, and when all the geese waddled into the pond for their morning ablutions, Pat and I hid in a nearby bush ready with some marker tags to see who was doing what to whom. In a flurry of spray it soon became apparent that they didn't really care. Ones that we had marked as being definitely female promptly launched themselves on the backs of others we had thought definitely females and vice-versa. Others, having finished mating one way, just swopped places and did it the other way. All we got was wetter and no wiser until mid-March when two of them started to lay eggs.

After the ducks, the way all the geese banded together to care for their eggs was a revelation. All of them, without exception, stood guard outside the shed in shifts, so that any attempt to count the eggs had to be done wearing stout clothing and gloves to guard against the vicious nips these birds can give one's backside and other extremities when caught off guard. But for all their devotion to duty, the numbers of eggs seemed to be declining daily without trace and it wasn't until we kept watch for most of one night that we came across the culprit - a black mink.

These ferocious little animals with their terrible beauty have become one of Ireland's main predators. With practically no natural enemies themselves, their spread has become swift and engulfing. One by one they removed the eggs until none was left and the disillusioned mothers had to wait another year. Pat built them a mink-proof cage, wired top and bottom, with strong locks into which the mothers were shut for the entire four weeks of their confinement, only emerging when the little ones were all hatched and fluffed up ready for the big, wide world. In the open the geese had a better chance against the mink, but we were still to lose several more to them over the course of the years. According to the bible, geese only eat grass all year, but can be caged and fattened up at Michelmas for a few weeks prior to slaughtering. The idea of deliberately caging the geese to fatten for the table seemed particularly inhumane after their onslaughts by the mink and we only ever killed one and ate it without much enthusiasm. Any thoughts you may have of abounding in feather pillows and duvets from the plucking take a bit of a knockback when it becomes apparent just how many geese you will need to pluck to fill one pillow. Our constant battle with the mink meant that our small flock never increased greatly in numbers and it wasn't possible just to eat all the surplus males as we never did learn to tell one from the other.

At the same time as we were struggling with the baby ducks and baby geese, it so happened that the children noticed baby turkeys for sale at Kenmare Fair one June morning. Although there is absolutely nothing whatsoever appealing about a baby turkey, it was the prospect of a free Christmas dinner that caught me momentarily off guard. Not intending to eat all four for Christmas, the terrible survival rate of the baby ducks and geese had made a deep impression by this time and the thought occurred that it was better to be safe rather than sorry. The notion that if you rear a bird yourself and then eat it means you get it for free is a total fallacy. Not only must you take into account the money you will spend on providing them with suitable housing, but also all the many sacks of food that they will consume between purchase and the table. You can console yourself that at least your free-range bird will taste better, but dwell for a moment on the fact that this could just possibly be wishful thinking by the way of compensation. There is also the added hazard of consuming something that you have spent the last five months chasing around the garden and is now staring at you from the plate. The self-sufficiency books make no mention of this and it is up to each individual to come to terms with his or her conscience.

But in spite of all these retrospective dire warnings, the baby turkeys came home with me that day. Pat was away on the rig so the turkeys were put into the chicken house, having first installed some lower perches for them as a temporary measure. Somewhat belatedly, the bible was then consulted and we were a bit taken aback to read that turkeys were very delicate birds, prone to all kinds of diseases and not recommended for the self-supporter in any way. It also said that they should be kept well away from chickens. Jason was hurriedly despatched into the night and dragged some rather surprised turkeys out of the chicken shed and threw them in with the ducks. The morning presented us with an even greater problem in that the chickens had the free-range of the entire neighbourhood, so we would have to confine either them or the turkeys.

In retrospect, there was no contest. We were to discover that not only did young turkeys have amazing flying abilities and take off for the woods on all possible occasions, but they were also particularly aggressive. The object of this aggressiveness was to be the children and they would quite happily attack them on sight, causing much mayhem and tears. So it was back to town again and we bought some wire netting and then had our first attempt at putting up fences. It's not easy to hammer a fence post into bedrock, especially when you are downright danger-ous with a pickaxe, but between us we managed to create some semblance of a fenced field. Luckily, there were no strong winds before Pat came home and was able to effect a more permanent structure.

Mark, who was now aged about five and a half, misin-terpreted the reaction of the turkeys and took their frantic rushings at the wire fence to be a sign of affection. He spent many hours sitting on our side of the fence chatting away to one particular turkey that he named Esmerelda and could not be persuaded that her ruffled feathers and murderous onslaughts were anything but signs of great af-fection for him and a quite definite love/hate relationship developed between the two. He would bring her handfuls of food consisting of anything he could find, such as bits of straw or apples or grass and bunches of flowers. She ignored all of these love tokens until one day he brought her some blackberries which she greedily ate on the spot. When eventually poor Markie tired of bringing endless supplies to her, she looked around to see if she couldn't find any herself. It didn't take long to finish the few that were in the field and for her then to spot the millions of others that hung, big and ripe and luscious on the other side of the fence. Getting at them presented no problem at all. She just went up to the top of the field, rushed down the hill with straggly wings outspread, and took off into the air. Having a swallow skim by you through the air is one thing, having a 20lb turkey do the same thing is another matter entirely. Luckily she missed, but it seemed prudent to lie quietly on the ground all the same, as the other three decided to follow suit. There then followed an orgy of blackberry eating which was to continue unabated all autumn, despite clipping their wings in an attempt to keep them grounded and in the field.

They were getting very large now and attempts to mimic a humming-bird halfway up a blackberry hedge more often than not ended in disaster. They would plunge to the ground in a mass of purple beaks and feathers, then crawl back out of the brambles and attempt to hover again. This gluttony was bound to end in disaster and, one morning in late October, one of the male turkeys misjudged his landing approach and flew straight into a tree. As he was almost fully grown and in the peak of health, it was decided to eat him, only to find after plucking that his flesh was a dark purple colour – just like the blackberries. Nobody could bring themselves to eat dark purple turkey, so he ended up being given to the dogs. Obviously, something had to be done to keep the turkeys confined. They had been travelling further and further afield in their search for blackberries new and, if they weren't found and chased home before dusk, they would just roost in the nearest tree. It got to the stage when Jason was spending about an hour each evening searching for them, so by the time Pat got home from the rig, he was informed by us in no uncertain terms that he would have to build a cage immediately to keep the turkeys in so that they would be fattened up in time for Christmas.

The finished cage was quite a work of art with its own

enclosed little turkey house and fine run outside. It also had stout wire netting above and below to keep the predators out and the turkeys in. Pat was well pleased with himself and stepped back to admire his handiwork. The other female turkey, who had been watching him during the day with interest, stepped into her new home, looked around and then promptly ate a half dozen nice shiny nails out of the box which Pat had left on the floor. She then keeled over and died on the spot. The dogs were delighted that Christmas had now come twice within a few weeks and we were left with the remaining two. Any thoughts of eating Esmerelda, who was by far the fattest after all her individual attention, went straight out of the window unless we were prepared to let Markie die of grief. So she got to have a month in the fattening cage and then waddle off scot-free, whilst as her remaining chum was a male, it seemed more sensible to keep him until the following Christmas and use him as a husband for Esmerelda. This way we would be able to save money on buying young turkeys and rear our own instead.

The bridegroom-to-be was named Clarence and a surfeit of food over the winter soon had him fattened up a bit. He was never to reach quite the same size as Esmerelda, although he spent most of his time strutting up and down in front of her displaying. Watching a male turkey display kept the children amused for hours. First, they puff up all their feathers, like a balloon filling with hot air. Then, as they continue to inflate, their heads start to go from pink, to red, to darker red and finally blotched all over with purple. The lump of skin on their foreheads grows longer and longer till it hangs over their beaks and when they finally reach bursting point, they open their beaks and gobble-gobble frantically, deflating as they go. It is the most amazingly ugly sight.

But for all his displays of unrequited love, Esmerelda was definitely not impressed and treated him with total

contempt. But Clarence was desperate by this time. He just had to have a mate. He tried leaping on a passing white chicken, but was savaged in mid-puff by the cockerel. Being smaller than Esmerelda, it was obvious that any attempt to leap on her was not going to succeed without her co-operation, which was definitely not forthcoming. So he finally resorted to trickery. Having taken note of the fact that Ezzy spent a great deal of time sitting in a dustbath, he also noted that the children had placed a milk crate alongside it in order to facilitate jumping over the fence. So he waited till she was happily sunbathing one day, sneaked up onto the milk crate and leapt on top of her. Success at last! Esmerelda was so flattened by this amorous weight falling from the sky, that by the time she gathered her wits about her, the deed was done. Due to the fact that Clarence was able to repeat his conquest several times in a similar manner, we were beginning to think that maybe Ezzy did sort of like it after all. Then, one day Clarence crept round the corner fluffed up and purple, hot with desire and there was Ezzy sitting on his milk crate. With nothing higher to stand on, the milk crate became a very effective method of birth control and subsequent general peace and quiet.

But frustration is a terrible thing and Clarence was definitely frustrated. Startled ducks and chickens, and even the cockerel, got really fed up with being leapt on at odd intervals, so he took to attacking the children. This was a bad mistake on his part as not only did he inflict several minor injuries, but it was just coming up to Easter. So Clarence ended up as Easter Sunday lunch and Ezzy immediately started to lay her eggs, now that she no longer had that dreadful fellow to bother her. The eggs, of course, were unfertilised and although one turkey egg makes the most marvellous omelette, we all felt very sorry for Ezzy when she started to go broody. With mothering instincts as desperate as Clarence's sexual ones, she sat on anything – duck eggs, chicken eggs (all of which got squashed under her weight), even stones – in her desperation to hatch something. Eventually we filled two of her eggs with pollyfilla, gave them time to harden and let her sit on them, hoping she would eventually get fed up or hungry when nothing happened. But Ezzy continued to sit with stolid patience. On Fair Day in Kenmare that July, there were the little ugly baby turkeys for sale again and it gave me an idea. Purchasing two, we crept down to the turkey cage very late one night, gently lifted up a rather cross and sleepy Ezzy, removed the two eggs and replaced them with the two eight-week old babies. Convinced she had hatched them herself, Ezzy took to her two new children like a duck to water and continued to rear successfully our Christmas lunch in this manner for many years to come.

6

MUD, MILK AND MIDGES

When you decide to make the progression from your domesticated pussy cat or dog to other larger and wilder animals, it is most important to bear in mind that they are just that. The second most important thing is that they take up a great deal of your time and, unlike small children when you have really had enough of them, you cannot farm them out to a willing neighbour with relative ease. Also, the number of babysitters who can also milk a goat are few and far between. Animals, like children, have pretty accurate internal clocks, will regularly show up at a certain time of day to be fed, milked, etc, and will happily hang around for the odd half hour munching on your flowers or vegetables (whilst you flag down the odd passing vehicle about ten miles from home trying to borrow a car jack to change the wheel, which someone has inadvertently used for something else). Then, after about half an hour they will wander off to greener pastures and you will get home tired, dirty, with a car full of shopping and screaming, equally dirty babies, and have to spend an hour or so scouring the mountainside in the gathering darkness or pouring rain trying to find them and drag them home again to be milked.

That's another thing about alternative animals: you need to be fairly strong. Running up and down mountains is something that will come naturally after a year or two, but pulling a reluctant goat, sheep or calf for several miles is another matter. Very quickly you will come to learn that they are definitely stronger than you and you will also realise that all animals are totally motivated by food. So the next time you lose one, make sure you always set off carrying a bucket of flake maize. This is a substance much like cornflakes in colour and general appearance, and there is yet to be discovered an animal that won't follow you to the ends of the earth, at any time of day or night, in order to get its head stuck in the bucket. The best thing is to throw out a handful now and then to distract it whilst you gain the odd precious few yards.

Now, with goats, it is very easy to find a good reason for keeping one. We lived about fourteen miles from the nearest town, there were no milk deliveries and most of the local farmers sent all their milk to the creamery lorry each day, or it became that time of year when the cows are 'dry'. Anyway, our milk supply was unreliable and erratic at the best of times and on top of this we had an extremely hungry new-born baby to feed, so a goat seemed the obvious answer. Of course, we had to have two – in case the first one got lonely – so we asked around locally and left messages that we were in the market for a couple of milking goats. It is surprising, even in the middle of nowhere, just how many goats are suddenly in need of a deserving home at prices ranging from the sublime to the ridiculous. The self-sufficiency book will tell you all about breeds of goats, the advantages between same, and what the modern, discerning goat buyer should look for. There are Saanens, which are pure white and give masses of milk; Nubians which have long, floppy ears and give rich milk in lesser quantities; and scrubby mountain goats, which will give you plenty of milk (unless you like to bath in the stuff) if only you can catch them.

The two we eventually settled on fell into this last category. True, one of them was white – perhaps a touch of Saanen – with brown shaggy patches and one horn and, although the other was black from the tips of her cloven hooves to her gleaming black eyes and horns, she did have one floppy ear. Anyway, it was the nearest we could find and they were reasonably inexpensive, which if we were truthful, was the major deciding factor.

When you look at your self-sufficiency book, you will find a picture of how to milk a goat. This, from various angles, will show you where to sit, where to put your bucket and how to place your fingers round its teats, and more importantly, it will show you the goat standing there meekly and quietly whilst this operation is carried out. The first thing you should realise is that unless you have bought a tame, hand-reared, dog substitute, goats do not stand still whilst you milk them. The first day we attempted to milk ours, we began with the white one which we called Bunny. She certainly looked quieter and older (more experienced perhaps?) than the other and, indeed, when she had her head in the bucket of maize, she stood reasonably still. If like us you haven't had the foresight to build a goat-milking stand as in the book, you have to get down on your knees in the mud, place your head in the goat's side and firmly grasp these enormous pendulous tits and squeeze.

The effect is astonishing. The goat will raise its head from the bucket, glare at you, quite deliberately kick you, replace its leg in the milk bucket – which will fall over – and then continue eating. If its head is not securely tied, it will also attempt to butt you with its horns, which is an even more astonishing experience. It takes many hours to get the hang of extracting the milk, during which time you

will get extremely hot, muddy and bothered. Every midge in the area will immediately gather and begin to breakfast on you. The goat will remain relatively unaffected. The trick is to learn to milk with one hand only. With the other, you can swat midges, keep a firm hold of the milk bucket and extract the goat's foot out of it every few minutes.

Whatever else happens, it is absolutely vital that you finish the milking before the goat finishes the maize. You must also make sure that the second goat, who is waiting to be milked, is securely tied at a good distance away and is also being fed. Otherwise it will decide that its sole object in life is to reach the food bucket of the first one. You will spend a great deal of money on sacks of maize, but it is all in a good cause. Do not attempt to get another person, or willing child, to keep a hold on the second goat. Goats are very determined creatures and are not discouraged easily. When you have finished milking the first goat, get up out of the mud with the bucket of milk that the first goat has stirred with its foot several times. Don't attempt to remove the swimming midges at this stage. Give the first goat more food and move on to the second one.

If you are unlucky, you will have a second goat like the one we named Magsie. She had absolutely no intention of being milked by anyone at all. She would feed from the bucket till you got within striking distance and then lunge out. We ended up tethering her to a five-bar gate. We tied her head to one bar, lashed her body to the gate and then tied her feet together in pairs. Then, with Pat leaning on her, we managed to extract about half a pint of milk. In the beginning the whole milking operation took two of us about two and a half hours and even several years later, when we considered ourselves to be experienced milkers, it would still take half an hour to milk them both. You end up with a bucket of warm, muddy, midgy milk which can easily be strained through a nappy liner whilst you take a much needed bath, should you then still have the time.

During these first days of becoming a goat owner, you will discover that goats have quite a strong smell. And you, having spent the best part of a couple of hours wrestling with them, will also have the same smell. You will not have time to endlessly bath or shower and wash your clothes, which will also pong. This is just something you have to learn to live with. On the positive side, the milk will not smell. All the tales you have heard about the taste and smell of goat's milk are really not true. If goats are running free on the mountainside and having a varied diet, their milk is lovely, especially chilled. Our children, who had not heard other people's misconceptions about goat's milk, accepted it cheerfully and never noticed any difference. It also makes the most marvellous yoghurt. The next problem to face is what to do with your goats when you are not wrestling with them. You must first make the decision between goats or a garden. If you have both, the first will eat the second. Fences are a minor irritation to a goat. We put up a six-foot-high stout fence around our

small patch and Magsie just hung around until the children
left the gate open one day and she just 'happened' to be
there. You will be quite amazed at what a goat can eat in
five minutes. Don't believe the old stories you hear about
goats eating all manner of things, like washing, shoes, etc.
It simply is not true. They only resort to things such as these
in the absence of anything else. And, believe me, there is
always something else, such as your vegetable garden, pots
of flowers on the window sills, your young tree you have
been giving such care and attention, etc, etc.

As we had rented thirty-six acres of scrub mountainside
with our cottage, the general idea was for the goats to graze
on the mountain and return twice a day to be milked. So
each morning after milking we chased them off up or down
the mountain, and each day they followed us back home
again. Goats are extremely curious and like to hang around
the place, taking careful note of what you have put where
and what you are doing. I can clearly remember Magsie
watching me hastily repairing a gap in the fencing around
our attempts at a vegetable garden, whilst she nonchalantly
stood munching on one of the other fence posts. As our
kitchen windows were at ground level, many an hour she
would stand staring at me through the glass, thinking evil
thoughts and happily chewing the cud in eager anticipation
of meals to come.

Goats can be tethered and the self-sufficiency books
advise a 'running tether'. This is an extremely long length
of extremely strong nylon rope, securely tied to something
extremely strong at both ends. You will discover which
type of rope is most suitable after your goat has eaten
through several varieties. You then place a collar on your
goat, a ring round the rope and attach one to t'other –
preferably with a chain. The running tether should be
reasonably taut about a foot above the ground where, it
is guaranteed, you will always trip over it. Even so, your
goat will spy something tasty which is not directly above,

below, or either side of the tether and attempt to get at it, winding the rope round several trees and bramble bushes in the process. There are times when you will simply have to tether your goat, but in the main goats and tethers are not compatible.

Our self-sufficiency book talked of housing for goats. You, like us, will go to a great deal of time and trouble constructing a raised goat bed in your shed, free from draughts (which goats hate) and rain (which goats hate even more), when in all truth the goats would be far happier living in your house with you. They will make this plain by attempting to nip inside the kitchen door every time you leave it open. It is easy for me to recall one particular instance which demonstrates this clearly. Markie came down with suspected meningitis the day before his fifth birthday. Pat was away on the rig, things were fairly chaotic at home, because not only was I up to my eyes in birthday cake, chocolate crispies and balloons, getting ready for the big day, but we were also looking after a very pregnant goat named Daisy, who hung around the kitchen door looking for love and sympathy. She belonged to friends of ours who were visiting relatives in England and, as she didn't have to be milked, it seemed unlikely that she could possibly be any trouble. Anyway, come the day before the birthday, Markie was so ill by mid-morning that it became necessary to farm the other two children out to a neighbour and drive him the fourteen miles to the doctor. He diagnosed possible meningitis which meant driving to the hospital in Cork some seventy miles away. Before leaving Kenmare, chancing to meet a good neighbour of mine embarked on her weekly shopping trip, the details of my predicament were explained over a cup of coffee. Not to worry she assured me, she and Jason would take care of the house, Gemma and the animals till my return.

Well, Markie was alright despite a sore back from the lumbar puncture and he recovered in a week or two. But

on the second day at the hospital (the actual birthday), a nurse brought me an urgent message to return home at once. What had happened in my absence was that, although Jason had carefully put all the animals away in their shed, the visiting goat had decided it was lonely, or something, got out of the shed, broken down the back door to the cottage and ensconced herself in the house. All the other animals in the shed had obviously decided then that our house was better than theirs and had moved in too. Jason and my neighbour were unable to remove the goat as they feared she might give birth on our fireside rug if provoked, so had phoned me.

Arriving back, tired from the long journey, it was like a scene from *Animal Farm*. The kitchen door leaned drunkenly on its hinges and the chickens perched amongst the jellies and chocolate crispies. The floor was awash with goat droppings, bits of dried herbs that the goats had pulled down and eaten, and lumps of birthday cake. A trail of disaster led through the house. The dogs were upstairs sleeping on the beds, all my plants and vases of flowers lay in pools of water on the floor half-eaten, and there in the living-room, eyeing me suspiciously, was our goat guest. She had knocked the television over in an effort to get to a more tender morsel of my hanging spider plant and was now lying on the rug surrounded by droppings, the odd cushion, bits of plants and pools of water. Not caring if she had quads en route, my outburst of temper was such that she got walloped repeatedly over the head with a rolled up newspaper, chased right out of the house and halfway up the mountain before she could get out of range. The rest of Mark's birthday was spent clearing up the mess and topped off by having to drive the seventy miles back to Cork to visit him cheerfully in the hospital.

After owning goats for a few weeks or months, you will begin to notice that your country cottage is beginning to look a bit like Colditz with the emphasis on stopping things getting in, rather than out. Having spent many a happy hour in the past looking at pictures of charming country cottages in magazines, their doorways surrounded by leafy clematis and fragrant jasmine and the cottage garden awash with multicoloured flowers, it now gave me cause to wonder idly what a goat-free existence must be like. But then, people who wish to be self-sufficient do not have time for beautiful gardens and the heady scent of roses. That's in another lifetime.

Anyway, back to reality and the goats. You will soon discover from your book that in order to have a plentiful supply of milk, you must get your goat 'in kid' each year. It's only the posh pure Saanens and Nubians that will give milk for two years without kidding. The scrubby mountain variety will give you plenty, and I mean PLENTY, just after kidding and this supply will slowly dwindle down during the summer until you are hard pushed to get a couple of pints a day. So it is important to make sure that in spring you get a decent cookery book that deals with meals made almost exclusively from milk products and encourage the little darlings to drink milk on all possible occasions. Six or eight litres of milk a day, every day, soon mounts up and cheese-making is not as easy as it looks and is very time consuming. Of course, you could always get a pig and feed the excess milk to it, but what do you do with a pig in the autumn when the milk supply dwindles and it becomes a choice of who gets the milk, the children or the pig?

Anyway, having changed your dietary habits to suit the milk supply, come autumn – the self-sufficiency book tells you – your goats will come into season. An experienced goat-keeper will be able to tell instantly whether a goat is in season or not. You will not be able to. The book tells you that the 'signs' are that they will make more noise and hang about the house more from September to February. Well, as your goats will already be making plenty of noise all day long and never have left the kitchen window since you got them, that is of no use to you at all. To make matters worse, they only come into season for four days of each month and are only 'receptive' to the Billy for twenty-four hours of these. The simplest way of being sure that your goat is 'covered' by the Billy is to put her with him for at least a month. In theory that is. In truth you will find that most Billy owners aren't too keen on keeping your little treasures for more than a day at the most. Try bribing them with money and, if this fails, invent a dying relative in some distant country that you must visit immediately, and appeal to their finer instincts. This however, will only work once and the next year you will have to find another Billy. For reasons which I will come to later, Billy owners are far and few between and always live miles away. Transporting a goat from a to b can be done in a car. In fact, one goat fits quite well into a VW Beetle in the back seat, but two do not. If you do not have either a car, tow bar or trailer at this point, either get one or find a friend with them. The first time we took Magsie and Bunny to be covered, we decided that to improve the breeding of the kids, the only proper husband should be Eros, a full-blooded Saanen who lived some thirty miles away across the mountains. In fact, we were pleasantly surprised at the way the two goats stood up on the trailer and seemed to take all the bumps and potholes in their stride.

On arriving at the farm far out on the Beara Peninsula, we found a note from the owners stuck in the door informing us that they had gone out for the day and to look on the mountain for Eros and leave the goats with him. All our good intentions about ensuring a proper introduction between our ladies and the gentleman promptly disappeared when Pat rounded a rock with Magsie and Bunny in tow and came in sight of Eros. His obvious delight in spotting the two ladies encouraged him to charge down the mountainside and Pat's reaction at seeing something the size of a small horse with giant horns descending upon

him with speed, encouraged him to release the goats and
beat a very hasty retreat. We left a suitable note in return
on the door to the effect that we would return in three
weeks or so, together with an envelope with some money
by way of encouragement, and went home.

A goat is pregnant for about five months, so if she gets
into kid in October, she will give birth in March. There are
signs which indicate whether she is in kid or not, but you
will find that due to the thick matted winter coat she has
grown to protect her from the elements, it is impossible to
tell. However, about two weeks or so before kidding, she
will start to obviously fill up with milk and you can then
make ready for the new arrivals. However, you should bear
in mind that no matter how enticingly comfortable you
make the goat shed with lashings of hay, buckets of water
and bowls of maize, the chances are it will be ignored.

Admittedly Bunny did give birth reasonably near to the
shed. The place she chose was right in front of the kitch-
en window, thus giving our children an instant lesson on
where babies come from and dispelling any notions they
might have had about storks and gooseberry bushes and
the like. It was a bit like watching a large television and
she didn't seem to mind the children's shrieks and giggles
at all. In fact, she promptly repeated the event and gave
birth to a second one about half an hour later.

Magsie, on the other hand, did nothing for about a
week, except grow larger and larger and more and more
cantankerous. She kept wandering further and further
afield, until she eventually gave birth to twins one morning at about 6.00am standing in the middle of a shallow
stream. It didn't appear to be the best of birthing places
and the first kid seemed to be distinctly upset at being
dumped in icy running water so soon after emerging, so I
attempted to drag her clear of the water, first moving the
kid on to the nearby bank by way of encouragement. But,
true to form, Magsie was not to be moved. She ignored

the first kid and despite my haulings and pleadings, gave birth to the second in the stream as well. Only then could she be enticed to bolt back up to the shed in pursuit of a bucket of maize, totally abandoning the kids and leaving us to carry them back up to her. She did, however, take motherhood reasonably seriously as long as we brought her regular meals at regular intervals.

There is nothing quite so delightful as new born goats, or kids as they are called. All of ours were snow white and could leap up into the air off all four feet at once. They were totally captivating and quite enchanting. We had just got around to deciding on names for them when, one morning, to our amazement and alarm we heard Magsie calling and making a great deal of noise around the house. Having got Jason out of bed, we dressed and went down to investigate further. She was alone, with no sign of the kids, and was obviously very distressed. With sinking hearts we combed the fields and mountainside. It didn't take long to spot the two little white bodies in the early April sunshine. Lying a few yards apart from each other, both had been savagely torn apart by a stray dog. It was one of the most horrific sights of my life. Jason, then aged about seven, took it in a calmer manner than me and together we buried them, making a small cairn out of a nearby stone wall. Children have a much more practical approach to life and death than we give them credit for, and do not grieve as long as we adults do. It was not the last time Jason was to be my support and help in times of drama.

Magsie, on the other hand, seemed quite deranged for a while and continued to call and cry for her kids in such a sad sound that it haunts me still. It was only when Bunny allowed her to become a kind of aunty to her two, that she seemed to get any kind of relief and begin to forget. Bunny's two kids were a male and a female. The self-sufficiency book said that if you did not intend to castrate any males and fatten them up to eat, you should put them down at birth. The little male kid was so appealing that there was no question of possibly eating it, and as Pat was away on the rig when they were born, there was no way on earth this repugnant job would fall to me in his absence. Then, after Magsie's kids were killed, any thought of his possible demise had long gone, so by the time Pat came home we had decided to keep them both. Alas, it was not to be. In order to stop him (and her) feeding off Magsie, whose milk we were now taking for ourselves, we tethered the two adult goats at some distance from each other and one day the little female got herself caught in the rope, lost her footing, and fell and broke her neck. As if that wasn't enough, a few weeks later we found the young male just lying dead in the field for no apparent reason at all.

It had been a tragic spring. However, the next autumn duly comes along, and in order to have milk, everything has to be repeated. During the following years, we did lose several more, but several survived. We had to become hard-hearted enough to have any male kids put down (by the vet) within twenty-four hours of birth and to learn the lesson that goats, especially the scrubby mountain variety, manage to birth quite well without your help and generally have a much longer survival rate if you just leave them alone to get on with it.

After a year or two, our major problem was finding a Billy in the autumn and we looked into the possibility of getting one for ourselves. After all, we could always get rich off his stud fees! As a well bred, fully grown Billy is extremely costly, we decided on a male about two years old that we knew had a foot infection and hence was being sold on the cheap. Our miles of open mountainside dealt with the pong – and do Billys pong! – but despite all our efforts, Danny as we called him, succumbed to the infection after about eight months and just before the mating season. One morning Jason came in and informed me that Danny was lying dead on the beach, this naturally occurring just after Pat had left for his month on the rig. It's hard to tell just how much a dead (or live) fully grown Billy weighs, but there was no way we were going to be able to get him back up the mountainside to the road and it really didn't seem too hygienic to leave him to fester on our one and only beach, so it was decided that we would wait until the tide came in, drag him into the water and let the tide take him away.

A marvellous idea in theory, but like all our good ideas, it was conceived without taking everything into account. Come afternoon and the high tide, Jason and I tied ropes around the unfortunate corpse and somehow managed to drag it up and down and over the rocks into the water. The tide then went out and just left Danny lying in a rock pool – admittedly a bit further out. Undeterred, we waited until the tide came in again, put the ropes back on him and then waded out as far as we could before casting off again. He floated out with the tide and we returned to the cottage jubilant, if not a little wet. As the tide came in again, there floating in on it right into our beach again, came Danny. By this time about two days had passed and what with being in the water, he was not a pretty sight. We waited for the tide again, put the ropes back on him and waded out, but this time good old Jason swam alongside him and I hauled from the rocks whilst he pushed from the water, and between us we took him about a mile up the coast. We were exhausted, wet and thoroughly fed up, but certain that Danny had gone for good. It just didn't seem possible when Jason called me the next morning and there, floating like an upturned boat on the tide majestically into our beach, was Danny.

It must have been this that finally caused me to break down and cry. But the cause was anger, not sadness, and in a furious whirl we set off down to the local pub, found a fisherman and paid him some of my precious housekeeping money to come round with his boat, rope the bloody goat, and take him as far out to sea as possible. Danny never did come back, but neither Jason or myself can pass that particular beach now without half expecting to see him come floating back in.

Eventually, after a few years, a dairy in Kenmare decided to start delivering milk to our local post office three times a week and, as our children did not suffer from any eczemas or allergies (for which goat's milk is excellent) the attraction of milk that came wrapped in a carton without any of the struggle became too much for us and we decided to make the change-over. But what to do with our own milk supply? The love/hate relationship we had over the years had somehow managed to make these two scraggy creatures part of our family and, as we felt quite certain that they were pretty well past their prime, we decided to set them free near a herd of wild goats that roamed the mountains several miles from our house. So we packed them in the back of the trailer again and set off. A flash of second sight made Pat carry them one at a time across part of a lake (goats hate water) in order to deter them from returning and it wasn't without the odd lump in our throats that we watched them wander off up the mountain.

We were never to see Bunny again, but the same could not be said for Magsie. About a year later we were all out in the car one day in that general area when we suddenly saw her. There she was, as large and black as ever, sitting in the middle of the priest's garden happily munching on his best dahlias. Our first reaction was to drive quickly past, but guilt got the better of us and we turned round and went back. Pat sneaked out of the car, grabbed her and much to her and their surprise, threw her in the back with the children and drove quickly home. We could only presume that she had come down from the mountains to kid, but it was not to be. After spending the winter with us and half the spring, we once more set out, carried her even further across the lake, and then took her even higher up the mountain before releasing her and she set off upwards again, without even a backwards glance.

Two more years passed and although we heard odd reports that she had been sighted here and there along the peninsula, she did seem to be heading away from us. Then one day, going on my weekly shopping outing into town and about three miles from our house, there she was, plodding steadfastly up the road towards us, with a baby Magsie in tow. Stopping to say hello to her, she immediately pushed her head in through the car window to check if by any chance I had a bucket of maize with me. Her disgust at finding that we no longer had the need to carry one at all times was obvious and she returned to the brambles. On my way home from town she was still there, heading in our general direction, so when school was over the long-suffering Jason set off on foot with a bucket of flake maize, whilst the rest of us brought up the rear in the car and brought a delighted Magsie, plus one, home with us again. Imagine our surprise when two days later a very irate farmer turned up at our house saying that we had stolen his 'valuable milking goat'. Trying hard not to laugh we handed her back over, and with a certain sense of relief, watched her disappear into the distance.

7

CALVES, SHEEP AND SHIT

Once you have got your cottage reasonably well fortified against goats, the wire fences are still standing and you have no flower or vegetable garden left to speak of, you may well be tempted to acquire other livestock. DON'T. You will reason with yourself that if you have to be tied to the house for one animal, you might as well be tied for several. RESIST IT. After all, you will say, you could be getting meat for the freezer at a snitch of a price. IT'S NOT TRUE. The chances are that if you were not born to farming and you have young children, ALL animals you acquire will be given names within hours of taking up residence and, once named, there is absolutely no way in the world they will make the journey from the field to the freezer. If you are 'so totally unthinking, uncaring and evil' (my children's exact words) to carry out this terrible deed, you will find that your whole family immediately becomes vegetarian and will refuse to eat meat of any kind just on the off chance that it might be Fred, Alice or Whomever and you will be left with a great mountain of meat taking up precious room in your deep freeze. But then again, if you ignore these words of warning, you will probably find out the hard way – like we did.

Our first venture, in aid of the freezer, was to buy two three-week-old calves. The local farmers spent several weeks beforehand advising us of the difficulties of rearing cows, but without a doubt, after having two goats around the house, calves are an absolute cinch! With an amazing touch of foresight we bought two little females (in case we should lose our good resolution over the years, we could always bath in milk) and the children named them Dolly and Daisy. Now, there are a great many different breeds of cows, some giving you more milk and some giving you more meat. But out here on the Beara Peninsula there are mainly the black and white variety called Friesians and this is what ours were.

We did initially consider buying the calves from the monthly cattle market in Kenmare, locally known as 'Fair Day'. This is a day of the month when all the farmers seem to take their cattle to town, regardless of whether they are planning to buy or sell them, and they gather them together in more or less orderly groups along the pavement. Any transactions that take place do so very early on and the rest of the day is spent in partaking of the odd one or two or three glasses of Paddy or Guinness and exchanging the news and the gossip with old friends and acquaintances. As the day progresses, the pavements become covered in piles of muck, the cattle become more and more restless, until they take to visiting each other as well and then the most wonderful chases ensue amongst the street traders, travellers, cars and passers-by. It's a day of organised chaos and really no place for the amateur buyer. The best place to go is to a local farmer who will have grown to accept your attempts at farming and from whom you will get a reasonable deal.

Now, the self-sufficiency book will tell you to mix up

a bucket of milk replacer for the calf. You can get this by the sackful and it closely resembles baby formula milk both in appearance and price. Having obtained the correct consistency and temperature, you grab the calf and place two of your fingers in its mouth. As with all babies, it will promptly start sucking and at this stage you push the calf's head – still with your fingers stuck in its mouth – into the bucket of milk, the theory being that it will then suck up the milk as well as your fingers. What the book does not tell you, is the method by which you get the calf to feed from the bucket without your fingers in its mouth before it becomes fully grown. Trying repeatedly to sneak my fingers out (which is no mean task as a tiny calf has a powerful suck), the calf just took its head out and looked around for my fingers again. Getting them to understand that milk did not come from my fingers took many weeks, but eventually this became a task which the children loved to do, and they only had to appear with a bucket to have the calves rush up to them and wonderfully loud, slurpy sucking noises would ensue.

It is necessary to issue a word of warning here: don't try to feed the calves anywhere near, or at the same time as, the goats. Animals are colour blind, so one bucket looks just as good and promising as another, despite the fact that it is filled with milk and not maize. A fight between a goat and a calf always ends up with the children in tears. In order to avoid this happening, and as Magsie was always lurking somewhere – just in case – the children took to feeding the calves just inside the kitchen door. This was also a mistake. It was alright when they were tiny – about the size of a large dog – but like all other babies, they have a tendency to grow, and a half-grown calf, or two, trying to fit into your kitchen on all possible occasions, is not recommended. Take it from one who knows.

As the days passed, Dolly and Daisy made the progression from milk to calf nuts without too much difficulty. By this

time they were about ten weeks old and quite irresistible. They followed the children everywhere and had the free run of what was left of the garden. Whilst they cavorted around the mountainside, us grown-ups faced up to the fact that serious alterations would have to be made to the house so that we could get in the doors without being accompanied by various animals, so a porch was built out of corrugated plastic sheeting and wood around the back door. Admittedly, it did keep the worst of the rain away from the house, and provided a great place to leave wet welly boots and coats. The cats thought it was simply marvellous – a custom built cat-house where they could stretch out on the shelves and sunbathe in peace and quiet, without the necessity of having to move when it rained. But it only took the animals a couple of days to negotiate two doors instead of one, and at best only meant a temporary delay to them.

Now you will find that animals don't move backwards too well and you have to turn them around before ejecting them. As our kitchen was long and thin, this necessitated a sort of eight-point turn with each calf, goat, etc. Unless you can achieve this without upsetting yourself or the animal in question, a spontaneous natural reaction takes place which requires cleaning up with a shovel afterwards, if you avoid treading in it at the time. The novelty of taking this out and placing in round the half-eaten roses pales after a bit. Indeed, it isn't long before the roses start to disappear under a great heap of it and unless you have had the foresight to plant them at least a hundred yards from the house, even you will start to notice the smell.

As house-training was out of the question, Pat made the unpopular decision that the calves would have to go and live in the fields on a permanent basis. The tears and pleadings and sour looks of the children were absolutely nothing compared to the reaction of the calves. They howled their heads off for what seemed to be weeks and when they did eventually calm down a bit and begin to take stock of their surroundings, it only took one of us to appear at the door to have them rushing back to the gate and start all over again. According to visitors we began to act very strangely. They couldn't appreciate why it was necessary to peep out of all of the cottage windows and then creep practically on all fours through the yard and the gate and down the road. As the sound of the car's engine was guaranteed to set them off for several days, a quick getaway was impossible and we couldn't all fit on one bicycle.

It was around about this time that we had seriously been considering the possibility of getting rid of our posh leased car. It was certainly very smart and very efficient during the floods, but really quite impractical for what it cost us each month. When you live an independent lifestyle, it slowly becomes obvious to you that outward appearances mean absolutely nothing. No amount of smart clothes, posh cars or the right accent is going to be of the slightest use to you when it comes to pushing a calf out of the kitchen and then slipping in the you-know-what and falling straight into it. The only thing that will improve is your grasp of some pretty explicit vernacular. You will get extremely fed up with polishing the children's feet each time you are about to get into the car, and bales of hay and straw, sacks of flake maize and the odd reluctant goat do absolutely nothing for the upholstery. Cars are just for getting from a to b, preferably without getting wet and without breaking down too often. You should be able to repair them easily yourself and they shouldn't go too fast, otherwise you will miss an awful lot of what is going on around you. Apart from scaring the birds, the animals and your neighbours, excess speed only means you are burning up large amounts of petrol, hitting the potholes harder and causing unnecessary damage to the road and the car. Indeed, it is probably the large, fast, shiny, four-wheel drive, camouflage-green variety that can be used as a rule of thumb to distinguish those playing at self-sufficiency from the deficient ones going about it in earnest. If you are going to attempt any sort of self-sufficiency, your car must contribute to and not be a drain on your daily life.

About this time it so happened that the neighbour who had sold us the calves in the first place had an estate car for sale. Not quite in her prime any more, she did have the odd fallen arch and could do with a touch of paint to cover up the rusty bits, but it was nothing that a few hours and lots of elbow grease could not put to rights. On the other hand, she had a few distinct advantages over our leased car or our bicycle. Being an estate, there was plenty of room for the children and one, or even two, goats. Negotiations were entered into and the result of these were that Dolly and Daisy were part-exchanged for the car and returned to live on the farm where they had been born. The children were placated with the knowledge that they could visit them whenever they pleased and that their future as milking cows was assured. Meanwhile, myself and Pat resolved firmly to cut down on our amount of animals, although we both missed Dolly and Daisy. If you had to rate the amount of effort against the amount of affection, they would have come out tops by a long way.

Although there are times when you may think you have left 'civilisation' far behind, it does have a nasty way of catching up with you and this was made obvious to us all when some lads attempted to break into our house one dark morning at about 3.00am. In country areas like this, the idea of locking up one's home like a fortress is quite laughable. As you are quite likely to be seven fields away or halfway up a mountain when someone comes to call, most people leave their key in the lock on the outside so that visitors can let themselves in and put the kettle on. In fact, we always had a good giggle at the tourists who carefully locked all the doors of their car before going into the pub for a drink.

So it was probably divine retribution that caused me to awaken that morning and hear the sound of somebody trying to smash the downstairs window. Putting my head under the pillow, my first reaction was to try and dismiss the sound as being something quite normal for that time of the morning, but breaking glass is breaking glass and it was quite obvious that there was no one but me to do something brave in Pat's absence to save us all. It's times like this that you get to realise what a coward you are. With precious seconds ticking away almost as loudly as the beating of my heart, it took all my earthly courage to turn the light on when, to my great relief, the would-be burglars made off into the night. Pepper, our bearded collie, who would quite happily sell his soul to have his tummy tickled, slept peacefully on, but Pat was not quite so happy on his return. He announced that I would either have to have a gun or a guard dog. Not only do guns terrify me, but the thought of having to keep the various bits of it all hidden away in different places so that the children couldn't assemble it for the odd game of cowboys and indians, made the whole idea ludicrous. Any burglar worth his salt would have had time to break and enter and remove the entire contents of the house before all the bits could be found and reassembled, let alone me ever getting up the courage to point it at him. So it would just have to be a guard dog.

Casper at nine weeks had lovely loose brown skin, four enormous feet, was about the size of a fully grown beagle and attacked the vet on sight when his innoculations were due. Pat and Grandma, who had brought him over from England, assured me that Rhodesian Ridgebacks would only ever attack lions or the odd wild boar, were strictly territorial and quite definitely family dogs. As we were a bit short on the former and he never did (or has since) show an inclination to stray further than the gate, this seemingly soppy guard dog became the next member of

our menagerie, despite the fact that his appetite threatened to bankrupt us all. The first obvious setback was when Pat came home and tried to get into bed on his next leave. It was at this point that Cassie decided to guard me to the death from this obvious invader and it took both of us and several bowls of food to entice him into the kitchen so that we could firmly shut the door and get some sleep. Pat spent many hours getting to know him and he slowly came to realise who this man was that came and went all the time, though any sudden move, such as an impromptu kiss or hug on Pat's part, often ended up with him being pinned to the floor.

As he grew larger and larger, his reputation spread before him and it must be admitted that although Pat assured me Cassie would never actually bite anyone, the sight of a fully grown Ridgeback coming straight at you in full cry could cause the stoutest burglar to waver. The trouble was that he treated all people, other than the children and possibly Pat, as potential burglars and our friends had to learn the need to stand perfectly still in the face of this onslaught whilst he ascertained if you were friend or foe. He became, and still is, one of the wonders of the neighbourhood and a burglar would have to come from far afield not to have heard of the fearsome enormous dog that guards us.

When Cassie was nearly six months old, he decided to attack a car in the road outside the house. It still is a debatable point which came off the worst. Unfortunately it was at the time when flu had got the better of me and the boys were at school, but the sound of screeching tyres and Cassie's yelping soon made me leap out of bed. The back door had been shut, and by the time it was opened by me, there was no sign of Cassie – just vast quantities of blood all over the place. The occupants of the car were alright and so after seeing to them, Gemma was bundled up and we set off to search for him. Despite his fearsome reputation, the local bush telegraph was soon at work, and shortly many people had joined in the search for the injured dog. Urged on by the vet, who assured us that a dog that large with internal injuries would drop within fifty yards of the accident, we hunted until dark trying to follow the trail of blood, but all in vain.

At first light, leaving the two little ones with neighbours, Jason and myself and other neighbours set out again as soft rain began to drench the hillside. With his razor sharp eyes, Jason quickly found a trail of blood which we followed for several miles, ending in a pile of crushed bracken where he had obviously spent the night. There the trail ended. Either he had cleaned himself up or the rain had long since washed all traces away. There was nothing for it but to just take the most logical way an injured dog would do. Then, as we debated what to do next, from round a gorse bush came Cassie, his front completely split open, revealing his breast bone, but still on his feet, though a trifle wobbly by this time. Somehow we got him down to the road and to the vet who spent several hours sewing him back together again. He marvelled at the fact that no bones were broken, but we felt that something more marvellous had happened. Neighbours and friends had given up their time to search for a dog reputedly fierce and dangerous, knowing it was injured, because they knew that we cared and suddenly that was the only thing that mattered.

When somebody, who also has children and has to face the inevitable, offers you a fully grown sheep for free, it's very difficult to stand by all your good resolutions and refuse it. Suddenly there are all kinds of good reasons why you need a sheep and even more suddenly, it's being off-loaded from the trailer and is standing around your yard looking hopeful. The first thing you must realise is the difference between all those pictures of little woolly lambs being cuddled and bottle-fed and the grown-up variety. They are like enormous, extremely heavy zombies. In twos or threes or packs they might well follow each other, but

in ones they don't. Not a glimmer of realisation seems to pass through those eyes as you scream, shout and attempt to push it out of the way. They are also very heavy and strong and do not like being carried. We found all these things out within about five minutes of his (her?) arrival. This time I was adamant – this sheep was strictly for the deep freeze and would have no name, no fuss and go straight out in the field. It didn't matter if it was a boy or a girl, it would stay until we had found the best method of getting it into plastic bags and, until then, it would be known as 'Sheep'.

You should bear in mind at this point just how ridiculous you will feel wandering round the fields looking for it and shouting 'Sheep' at the top of your voice. You will do this searching because unlike all other animals, sheep take no notice of fences – they just march through them. Admittedly our fences weren't the greatest. Fencing thirty-six acres for two goats who took not a blind bit of notice of them, and two calves who only ever strayed half a dozen yards from the gate, was not always our top priority. So there were the odd one or two places where the wire leaned a bit, or the stone walls had been demolished by the constant patter of little feet who couldn't be bothered to use the gate. Sheep would just set off in a straight line, munching away and slowly disappearing over the blue horizon. As she/he didn't ever do anything exactly spectacular, we would tend to forget about her and every few days there would be a frantic search over the hillsides. Now there are usually a lot of sheep on mountains, and telling one from the other is not for the amateur. After about forty-six, they all seem to look very alike and you begin to understand why somebody had the bright idea of counting them in order to fall asleep. They also don't answer to their name when called – or maybe that was just because standing in the middle of the odd hundred and shouting Sheep is enough to leave anyone wondering. But eventually some long-suffering farmer will inform you that your little treasure is causing chaos amongst his and would you please come and remove it. Then it's back to the problem of how to persuade a sheep to get in a car.

The days lengthened into weeks and then into months and Sheep didn't seem to be making any progress towards those plastic bags. Pat had been making various mutterings about shearing and dipping and such things and reading the self-sufficiency book with more than usual zeal. Finally he announced that he was going to shear Sheep on Tuesday next and, as it would be a difficult job, he was going to enlist help from one of his friends. However, you will find that whenever you make such an arrangement with a friend, because of the nature of things here, it is necessary to carry it out on the day arranged and the fact that on Tuesday next it was pouring with rain was no deterrent at all. As there was not enough light in the shed to see properly, there was no reason at all why it couldn't be done in the kitchen.

Whatever pictures you have seen in the past of strong bronzed men shearing sheep in about forty-five seconds flat you should remove from your mind at once. Sheep took great exception to coming in the kitchen in the first place and achieving this took two fully grown men half an hour and most of their energy. Pat had borrowed a pair of hand shears and had sharpened them up and I stood at a suitable distance, ie perched on the draining board, and read the instructions from the bible. The first thing to do was to pick her/him up and sit her/him down on her/his rump and clip the wool from the stomach. This was when panic set in and when sheep panic they wee all over the place. The two men struggled and slipped in the wee, bits of wool flew all over the place and the smell was beyond belief. The shears were abandoned in favour of my best sewing scissors and after a great deal of sweating, swearing and struggling on the floor, Sheep emerged looking like a terminal case of mange. The fleece, instead of being in one piece like your typical fireside rug, was in a hundred-million pieces, all either floating around in the air or floating on the floor in the you-know-what.

The men were only fit for the nearest bath and it took me several·weeks to both clean the kitchen and start talking to Pat again. He was a bit more subdued about the dipping bit and ended up chucking a bucket of foul smelling dip over Sheep one day as she ambled past. It didn't really come as any great surprise to me to find him loading her up one day into the back of the car and telling the kids how Sheep was going to live in a far, far better place. . ! At least he hadn't turned over the page in the self-sufficiency book which showed in graphic detail how to kill, skin and disembowel your sheep, though maybe my hiding the book safely away in the goat shed had something to do with that. Sheep did eventually come back in those little plastic bags, but she/he was never to grace our table. We had the everlasting memory of do-it-yourself sheep shearing to thank for that, but luckily Casper didn't seem to mind at all.

8

A TURBULENT MISTRESS

Despite the fact that Pat spent every other month on an oil rig surrounded by water, this in no way diminished his love and fascination for the sea, and his eyes would mist over with a faraway, glazed look whenever he looked at it. At the age of fourteen he had been working as cabin boy amongst the ice and storms of the Arctic Circle and then spent ten years tramping round the world on the ships of the Merchant Navy. The danger and the hard work he had endured for this watery Lady had resulted in a respect and devotion that was to become etched into his very being. Like all true fishermen, the sea was his mistress and his obsession for her was something that landlubbers like myself just had to learn to live with. Before we had come to Ireland this had been no great hardship as it had only meant the occasional day sunning myself on the river bank whilst he struggled to remove its contents. Fish was either something that came in neat, prepared lumps or, very occasionally in a rather flabby, slightly smelly, disembowelled state from the fishmongers. In my childhood I had been mackerel fishing a couple of times and the sight of those beautiful rainbow-coloured bodies threshing around in the bottom of the boat had ever so slightly tainted the excitement of the catch for me. A few thousand sea-urchins on our arrival in Ireland had really done nothing to improve matters and if it hadn't been for our enforced poverty, probably nothing would have changed me for all time.

But fishermen or not, there was no denying that living right beside the sea there was a source of unlimited free food right on our doorstep. At the age of five, Jason could spot the difference between a live or dead scallop lying stranded on the beach at low tide and spent hour after hour down amongst the sand and rocks gathering mussels, cockles, clams and anything else that looked remotely edible, and then bringing them home for me to cook for his tea. I drew the line at limpets, but he would just wait patiently till his Dad got home and then they would cook them up together and eat them with great exclamations of delight. Little Markie at two and a half was an entirely different matter and, on catching sight of the sea, showed a marked tendency to follow immediately in Dad's footsteps except that he didn't wait for a boat. His little eyes lit up and when he saw the water, he would just march on in – repeatedly, and usually fully clothed. He could spend the best part of a day just lying by a rock pool totally hypnotised by the contents and also totally unaware of the fact that the tide came in and out.

He learned this last lesson the hard way when one day Jason and I were out along the beach looking for mussels and Markie was lying on a rock sticking out of the shallow water gazing in wonder at the vast shoals of mullet that were lazing in the warm, calm water. These fish gather in their hundreds, fins sticking right out of the water like miniature sharks and show no great urge to rush off even if you walk in amongst them. Now I knew that the tide was coming in, but Markie didn't, and slowly the water crept further and further up his small island until the fact that it was lapping around his recumbent body dawned on him. He scrambled to his feet and shouted to me, but we pretended to be out of earshot and continued our wanderings. When the water reached his ankles he made an attempt to get off the rock, but by this time he realised he would be out of his depth, so he clambered up again and screamed and yelled at me. Difficult though it was at the time, I managed to ignore him until the water had crept up to his knees and then, and only then, did I effect a rescue. Thus Markie learned about the tides and I never had to worry about it again.

Although it may seem hard at the time, when your children are free as air to ramble where they please, it is very important that they are aware of a few basic rules. So far, not one self-sufficiency book we have come across seems to acknowledge the fact that children exist at all, let alone the fact that they may be small enough to have to accompany you at all times wherever you are going and whatever you are doing. They make no mention of the fact that even the simplest of tasks can be made far more difficult and dangerous by the presence of one, two, three or more youngsters that you have to keep half an eye on whilst the other half is on the job in hand. Being a grass widow for a total of half the year meant that it was necessary to have a sound plan of action for any emergency and allow enough time for any job to include having the children around. We had no ready babysitters and one of the most important lessons the children had to learn was that their freedom was bounded by small rules – and heaven help them if they strayed from the straight and narrow! As the children get older and more inclined to stray further afield, a good rule of thumb is to have a check-in time twice a day when they must physically present themselves in front of you to confirm that they are still alive and well. A good watch is essential for this: one that is shockproof and, especially in Markie's case, waterproof as well.

On his return from the rig, Pat was delighted to hear that Markie now knew about the tide waiting for no man (or small boy), but he was twice as interested to hear about the mullet down by the shore. After several attempts to catch them with a fishing rod which they studiously ignored despite the most tempting of bait, he decided to resort to a net. Deep discussions with the local fishermen revealed that they never caught or ate mullet, but they did end up giving Pat an old, discarded net which he proudly brought home.

Unless you have had previous experience, the sheer size of a fishing net is quite amazing. Ours was over a hundred feet long, of which about thirty feet was net and seventy feet were holes which took Pat well over two weeks to mend. By this time, having it strung up outside off the trees, all the non-fishing members of the family were beginning to get quite fed up with it. Chickens, ducks and turkeys were constantly getting stuck in it as well as the odd cross goat, so that by the time he lugged it down to the sea, we were all very glad to see the back of it. But with endless patience and ignoring our rude remarks, Pat waited for the tide to go out and then strung the net between a small offshore island and the beach. He was up and gone at first light the next day, and when he hadn't returned by breakfast time, we set off down to see what was holding him up. To me it looked as if he had caught every mullet in the sea, but in truth there were probably about three hundred ranging in size from about half a pound to monsters of over 10lb in weight. There were also two dead cormorants who had come to grief whilst attempting to dive for the netted fish and a variety of crabs and seaweed and also several more large holes where it had been necessary to cut the net to remove all the contents.

We were beginning to learn another lesson not mentioned in the self-sufficiency books and that is that food from the wild tends to come in large amounts or not at all. In your vegetable garden, either all the carrots are ready at once, or in spring you suddenly have gallons of milk and millions of eggs. This also applies to fishing. In olden days the housewife would have smoked or salted all the fish to preserve them, whilst today we resort to the deep freeze. All the same we had to face the facts that three hundred fish wouldn't fit in our deep freeze and we had managed to catch a variety that nobody else would eat. The main reason for this was basically a sound one as grey mullet graze in a cow-like fashion on seaweed and the like, and as they prefer warm water, they tend to congregate in shallow, possibly polluted water or places where warmer water is entering the sea, such as the outlet of sewage pipes.

But here along the south-west coast of Ireland, the waters are still as clear and unpolluted as they were meant to be, so for the brief few years before 'civilisation' catches up with them, the mullet remain quite delicious and free from nasties. So we squashed as many as possible into the freezer, gave as many as we could away and had to consign the remainder back to the sea from whence they came. It really then seemed quite incredible to me when, about two days later, there was Pat setting off to put out the net again, though luckily mullet are smart enough to re-route themselves after being trapped – that is, if there were any left alive to re-route.

There is really nothing quite like success and definitely nothing quite like a successful fisherman. Every fish in the sea becomes a personal challenge and eventually you will succumb to the endless rational arguments about the logic of owning a boat. After all, a boat will mean you can have your deep freeze crammed full of fish all year and you won't have to bother buying meat because there won't be anywhere to put it. In just a few years, this unbelievably expensive pile of wood, broken planks and peeling paint that looks just like a wreck to you will have paid for itself – that is, if you don't outlay too much money on making it waterproof again. But once you realise that you are expected to be the 'crew', somehow things like copper nails and chlorinated rubber antifouling paint will seem absolutely vital.

If being a boat owner is a whole new experience for you, and you are prone to seasickness like me, there are a few hints I can give in order to retain your sanity. The first, and most important, is NEVER learn to row. Co-ordinating two extremely long and heavy lengths of wood bears no resemblance to the pictures you have seen on television of Henley Regatta. If you learn how to row, the fishermen will soon have you rowing halfway to America whilst they just have one more go for that mackerel, pollock or mullet. Learn to bail instead with a steady repetitive motion. This has a wonderful psychological effect as it implies the boat is steadily filling up with water and may result in it being turned round towards land. It doesn't actually matter if there isn't any water, just keep bailing. Always take a good picnic and several thermos flasks of hot soup and lots of big, black plastic, dustbin liners. You will find the latter invaluable because it is invariably the case that those who are not doing the fishing always sit in the part of the boat where the waves and spray break over them. A hole made in one end and placed over your head will not look terribly elegant, but it will keep the three sweaters, T-shirt, long-johns, jeans and anorak you are wearing dry.

Sitting in soggy, damp clothes for hour after hour may seem totally ridiculous to you, but it is all part of the joy of fishing. If all else fails, you can always resort to seasickness, and beg to be taken ashore. However, it bears mentioning that here in south-west Ireland, as well as in many other parts of the world, it is considered 'bad luck' by local fishermen to have a woman in the boat at all. Several (female) friends of mine have come across this phenomenon personally. One, no less than an inspector of those vast ships that make their living fishing the icy wastes at the top of the world, was first refused permission to come on board, and having insisted and carried out the inspection, watched the captain issue orders for any place where she had stood on the deck to be scrubbed clean! How's that for superstition?

Closer to home, there are wives of fishermen who have made the odd disparaging remark about the lack of catch, spending the rest of the day trudging ten miles back home. So do make sure you have an intimate knowledge of the coastline before demanding to be put ashore and that you are reasonably near to a road where you can hitch a lift home without having to climb over too many hedges and cross too many bogs with the children. It's still a puzzle to me why sea-fishing remains such a male chauvinistic preserve, especially in view of the fact that they refer to the sea as 'She'. Maybe unlike you, She is that intangible being – the Perfect Mistress. Or perhaps you just don't have the time to be one.

Our own personal wreck consumed many hours and lots of money and was eventually converted into something seaworthy. She was twenty-three feet long and looked like a large rowing boat to me. She probably would have been a large rowing boat if neighbours hadn't been kind enough to lend us an engine, for which they have my eternal thanks. Life-jackets were purchased for the children at vast expense, although none was ever purchased for us. Pat is one of those swimmers who can swim steadily on for mile after mile and actually enjoy it. Although having always considered myself a reasonably competent swimmer and perhaps able to swim four or more lengths of the swimming pool, if dumped in the sea anywhere over fifty feet from the pier, I would probably drown, especially as Pat would be busy rescuing the children at the time.

If you are thinking of saving money on your own life-jacket, next time you go out to sea choose a choppy, grey, windy day. Next, try looking at the shore and estimating

if you could possibly make it that far . . . then go back to
the shop immediately. Whilst Pat got 'the feel' of the boat,
the landlubbers were left at home, but like a boy with a
new bike, he couldn't wait to show it off to us for long and
guess who was selected to be the first passenger? We went
out to check the old net which he had laid even further out
to sea in the hope of catching some more mullet unawares.
As he hauled the net in it got heavier and heavier to drag
over the side and, being told to lean out the opposite side,
as one does in a sailing boat, Pat did nothing to calm my
growing fears that it was nearing time to abandon ship. It
became increasingly obvious that he either had all the rest
of the mullet in the sea or something else equally heavy. It
turned out to be the latter – a dead, fully grown seal. The
poor thing had become entangled in the net and drowned.
Most people on seeing a dead seal about to come up over
the side into the boat would have taken action to release it
and commit it to the waves, but not so Pat. He struggled
gamely on until it was on board with us and taking up
most of the room. Whilst trying to scramble out of the way,

my subconscious became dimly aware of the remarks Pat was making how much oil there was in one seal. Visions of endless saucepans of seal blubber simmering away on the range got the better of me and I mutinied. It was either me or the seal going over the side right there and then and Pat (albeit with a touch of reluctance, it seemed to me) chose the latter.

The children took to the boat like ducks to water and were able to help Pat with many different methods of fishing. Our ninety-ninth hand, very mended lobster pot resulted first in a large eating crab and eventually in two lobsters. The first problem you have to face with such crustaceans in your kitchen, is that they are alive and quite definitely stare at you with reproachful looks as the water heats up in the saucepan. If you are able to overcome this and cook them, then you next have to find out how to remove them from their shells without skinning your fingers and removing what is left of your fingernails; but there is nothing quite so delicious as sitting down to 4lb of lobster cocktail between two of you and trying to eat the whole thing at one sitting. Because of the infrequency of either the weather or the situation being suitable for catching, it wasn't a problem we faced too often.

The children devised many methods of catching shrimps and prawns from the rock pools down by the beach, but after saving them up in the freezer for a week, we still only had the odd half pound in total. This was all to change when by chance one day, Pat happened to see a small French boy fishing for prawns down by the pier with an unusually shaped net and being extremely successful with it. So he rushed home and set about building one for himself. It consisted of a large wooden frame in the shape of a circle cut in half, the cut, straight side, having a long wooden handle attached to it. From the frame hung a net, which was lined with another very fine net, the idea being that you stood in your boat next to the pier walls and scraped the frame up the side of the walls, so that all the prawns happily dropped off into it.

Naturally, Pat built his frame four times the size of the one the small boy had and managed to construct it out of all sorts of odds and ends, except for the fine lining mesh. Getting a sudden demand for net curtains or something similar met with little response from me because although we had replaced the sacking curtains in the cottage with more normal ones, we definitely had no net ones. Although the request soon dimmed in my memory, Pat continued to root around the cottage until he eventually came up with the perfect answer – my wedding veil. Although it probably would never see the light of day again, it had been put away alongside the dress with not quite a dry eye and a care that only loving memories can bring, so it came as a bit of a shock to the system to see it being cut to pieces with the scissors in order to be part of a shrimp net. But this is another lesson in self-sufficiency not often mentioned – the need to be able to substitute creatively with what you have to hand. With the nearest shop being miles away, so you cannot nip in for the occasional DIY this and that, you need to evolve some pretty good lateral thinking and effect at least a temporary repair until further help can be got. So it is wise not to become too attached to any personal belonging, as it is just as likely to end up somewhere else when the need arises.

The completed frame was extremely heavy and very large and when Pat got into the boat and tried to drag it up the wall of the pier, all that happened was that the boat moved sharply backwards and the frame (and very nearly Pat) fell in the water. This was solved by attaching a rope to each end of the boat and Jason and myself hauling on the ropes against the push of the boat. Our hard work was rewarded with not only a great deal of seaweed, but also about 2lb of prawns per haul. We were all quite wrecked by the time we had covered the entire length of the wall and it was probably sheer spite that made me force Pat to sit up till 3.00am peeling the great mountains of prawns that we had caught.

Our next experiment at different types of fishing involved what is called a long-line. This is exactly what it says it is – a long fishing line with loads of hooks attached to it. These all have to be baited and then it can either be laid across the beach at low tide or, as in our case, set out from the boat. Some of the mullet came in useful as bait when cut up into small chunks, though baiting and coiling up the long line is not a job for the amateur as it does need to uncoil and go over the side of the boat with equal ease. The logic in taking the fish out of the freezer to catch more fish tended to evade me, but any such thoughts were swiftly dismissed when Pat told me that long-lines always catch something – and indeed they did.

Our first attempt presented us with about forty dogfish and twenty ray. The dogfish looked exactly like small sharks, and indeed do belong to the shark family, and are more commonly found in fish-and-chip shops calling themselves rock salmon. They are quite delicious and ideal for fussy children as they only have one bone inside them, ie the backbone. There is just one problem with dogfish not mentioned in the self-sufficiency books, and that is getting to the flesh. When you first pick one up you will discover why their skins are used for French polishing. This is because they are like fine sandpaper and do a great job of sanding your fingers unless you happen to be wearing gloves at the time. Pat picked up each fish, slit it around the head with a sharp knife and then pulled the skin down off the fish with a pair of pliers. When attempting a similar operation, my only result was to get very cross and rather mucky. No amount of pulling on my part would induce the skin to come away from the flesh, so dogfish could only be eaten during the time Pat was at home.

The ray, or skate, was a completely different problem.

The majority of them were about two feet across or more and if you measured to the tip of their tails, they were probably about two feet long also. None of my cookery books mentioned what to do with an entire ray, so it was necessary to consult the locals down at the pub. Cut off the wings, they told me, and either bury them in the garden or hang them outside for two weeks. The idea of burying them indefinitely in the garden had a certain appeal, but the thought of digging them up again and then cooking them was just not on, so it had to be the second alternative of hanging them up in the porch and there they stayed for two weeks. Once you have had to face the sight of ray wings every time you open the door, you won't feel much like eating them. Even the flies won't go near them. So the wings were consigned to our rapidly enlarging cats and requests were made to Pat to give any subsequent catch away to the locals. It probably is really quite delicious if you can get it as far as the table, but it requires a stronger stomach than mine.

Then came the day when Pat announced to us all that the gannets were diving and this meant the shoals of mackerel were moving into the bay. At last a chance to put some of my own experience (albeit in my dim, distant youth) into practice. The geese were raided for feathers, mackerel lines were made up for all of us and we set off out for a day's fishing. Now to me, the words 'a day's fishing' means that one continues to fish until you have caught enough to eat, and then you return home. To a fisherman, 'a day's fishing' means exactly that. From the first light of dawn streaking over the horizon until the last rays of the sun are well into the sea and all the time in between. It becomes a sort of contest between the man in the boat and the blue water to see if all the fish therein can be moved from one place to the other. Admittedly, the children were very excited at catching their first mackerel and there were soon great contests going to see who could catch the most – with mother trying to keep separate piles of them in the bottom of the boat. The trouble began when Gemma wanted to go to the toilet and refused to go over the edge of the boat saying, which seemed quite reasonable to me, that it was alright for the boys, but she might fall overboard. Their retorts did nothing for women's lib, and it was only when her crying reached hysterical proportions that Pat put into shore and us girls nipped behind a convenient rock. Our big mistake was to then get back into the boat, because the next time he put into shore was after dark. Even the boys had got fed up after lunch and my general demeanour had not been helped by being sick twice. My stomach had been alright whilst the engine was going and the boat moving, but all this drifting around on top of the fish made the height of the Atlantic swells become very obvious. When we eventually got home, tired, dirty and wet, there were then great piles of mackerel to be gutted and cleaned and Pat was really quite surprised when nobody wanted any for tea.

While Pat was away on the rig, it seemed like a good opportunity for me to have a go with the fishing rods myself. There was a place on the beach where the rocks suddenly rose sharply into the air, making a small cliff about ten feet out of the water. With a great effort of will-power, somehow it was possible for me to stand on the top of this, and with the children safely out of the way further down the beach, practise my casting. It wasn't long before a few suicidal mackerel got hooked and then some pollock and one garfish. The latter is a slim, silvery eel-like fish with a very long pointed nose. Certain we had caught some great rarity unknown to fishermen over the ages, we deep froze it in case the nation wanted to keep it for posterity, but on finding out from Pat that it was only a common garfish, we grudgingly gave it up as bait for the long-line.

On the beach, the children found they could catch little rock fish and shrimps with their hands, though Pat

soon put a stop to this as several varieties of rock fish have poisonous spines on their backs and can give quite a nasty sting. He much preferred that we spend our day cycling down the three miles to the pub to check that his boat was alright and didn't need bailing, so the children were forced to practise their hand-catching techniques on the small trout that lived in a nearby stream.

It had been the lure of the King of Fish, the salmon, that had originally inspired Pat to come to Ireland and the days that were too grey and mucky for sea-fishing proved to be ideal for river fishing on several of the marvellous rivers that twist and chatter and gurgle their way down to the sea around here. The children were instantly banned from this occupation as total silence is necessary. This effectively meant my being banned too, until such time as all the children were safely at school for part of the day. Although not half as prolific as sea-fishing, when he did catch either a salmon or a sea-trout, first its photograph had to be taken for posterity and then there was great celebration all round. The season opens here on St Patrick's Day (17 March) and if Pat chanced to be home on that date, nothing was allowed to stand in the way of catching the first salmon of the year which he did several times. He would be dropped off in the morning by the river and then we would return to get him after the kids came out of school.

One day, as we got to the appointed meeting place, we had just got out of the car when Pat hooked into a salmon and, for the first time, all of us got to witness the struggle between man and fish. All thoughts of keeping quiet were abandoned as the minutes passed and the children rushed up and down the bank imploring Pat to jump in after the fish in case he got away. It didn't, of course, but we all had a sneaking suspicion that he just might have jumped in if it did!

The second occasion when we were all to be together

in the presence of these mighty fish was one of those little time-warps when you see or experience something that is so stupefying and overwhelming that it remains close in your memory for ever. After the rain-free summer of 1984 when this little corner of the world began closely to resemble Spain with the soil turning to sand and the mountains caught in the eternal shimmer of a heat haze, a local fisherman happened to mention to Pat that there were 'thousands' of salmon down in the nearby salt lakes. Now even a fisherman knows that another fisherman is prone to exaggeration, so we took no notice until, wanting to walk off the effects of Sunday lunch, we clambered down the steep wooded slopes to the salt lakes. There, trapped by the drought and waiting for the rain to provide enough water for them to travel up-stream to the lakes, hundreds and hundreds of salmon and sea-trout had gathered to wait in the warm, salty waters of these seabound lagoons. We witnessed layer upon layer of fish lying right up to the shore, and at one point it was possible to see up to eight fish on top of each other before the others were lost in the blue depths of the water. The children could put their arms in and actually touch them because there was nowhere else for them to go. But alas the season was just over, and even if one had wanted to poach just a few, that night the sky trembled from the thunder that echoed back and forth amongst the mountains and the heavens opened to give those beautiful fish their escape up-river to the lakes where they would start the whole life cycle all over again.

Not only did the sea give us these once-in-a-lifetime experiences, but also more commonplace ones, such as the many seals whose curiosity would overcome their fear so that they would come close into the beach and watch the children watching them. We would hide and watch the shy otters playing in the kelp and sliding over the rocks on the beach, or marvel at the dolphins as they leapt out of the water chasing the elusive salmon down the Kenmare

River – always a sign of a good summer according to the locals. Even on the stormy, windswept days in the depths of winter, when the waves lash into the rocks and the spray covers the whole beach in a fine mist, you can run along with arms outstretched, challenging the wind to blow you over. On calmer days the rocks and rock pools provided worlds within worlds. Young eels could be caught from under them and crab races held on a patch of sand or mud. On summer days we could swim amongst the mullet, with Casper swimming alongside taking great mouthfuls of water just when he thought he had a fish within his grasp or lie, sunbathing, on a rock leaning against one of the goats for a cushion. It was easy to admit that this watery Lady, who inflicted her moods upon us all, well deserved that faraway look in Pat's eye, and perhaps he had caught the rest of us up in her magic spell of enchantment too.

9

THE WILD AND THE FREE

One of the first things you will notice upon coming to live in the country is just how much sky there is. With no buildings to block your view, you will very quickly become aware of this magnificent panoramic spectacle of clouds and colour that is put up in front of you for free every day. When you go out in the boat, this will give you yet another perspective of things, and that is how different the land looks from the sea and the overwhelming immensity of them both. No visit to any planetarium can prepare you for just standing outside on a clear night and seeing all those stars through a clean, unpolluted atmosphere. If you have leanings towards religion, this will be the time of your wholesale conversion. If you do not, you will probably buy a bicycle. Mainly because on a bicycle you can move relatively easily and almost silently through this whole marvellous spectacular extravaganza. If you are also a touch unfit and find yourself pushing the bike up every tiny incline after the first invigorating mile, in order to take your mind off the pain in all those muscles which you never knew you had, you will begin to notice that there is yet another whole new world out there. This is the world that is missed by the car as it rushes past or the train thundering along on its tracks. It's just the world of dead leaves, the first violet of spring or a tiny, sparkling stream that go to make up the total canopy of colour stretching to the far horizon. Slowly and steadily your eyes will begin to open to things you have heard about, but never actually seen before.

When Jason first started school on our arrival at Fairy Pass, it was during the time that we had no car and only one child's bike. As it was four miles to the door of the school and four miles back again, the thought of walking all that way dragging a reluctant pupil was horrifying so we borrowed a bicycle. Unlike your modern ten-speed racer, this was a large, old, black thing called a 'Sit-Up-And-Beg' variety that stout-hearted mothers were to be seen cycling about on during the Blitz. But it had a child's seat on the back and a touch of oil diminished most of the squeaking noises. If you haven't actually been on a bicycle since you were a teenager, the first few days will come as something of a shock to the system, especially if you have to carry a heavy four year old on the back which means you can't topple into the brambles when nobody is looking. Taking him to school this way for the first time, my pounding heart and wheezing breath, combined with the urge to remove all my clothes on the spot, made it seem as though life was dripping out through me in the drops of sweat.

Although this tenuous cycling ability slowly improved, these daily trips to and from the school were the first contact with the fact that we were heathens living in a predominantly Catholic country. The local school and others like it had been Catholic since time immemorial and any matters pertaining to the running of the school were therefore given out at Mass on Sunday. These matters included such things as sudden days off given in a moment of geniality by a visiting Bishop or certain Saint's Days that Catholic custom denoted should be school-free. As a small four year old is not a very reliable rememberer of messages and no notes to such effect were ever given and if, like us, you were of the heathen variety and did not attend Mass, you remained ignorant of such matters. On more than one occasion, having struggled all the way to the school, it came as something of an anticlimax to find it shut and my subsequent mood and language did nothing towards a possible conversion. It was only when my next door neighbour's children became of school age and she was kind enough to take the trouble to pass on these dates to me that matters improved.

Self-sufficiency books make no mention of religion or adapting to the ways and customs of another area – presuming, of course, that you had to move in the first place to change your way of life. Getting this close to the ground is a moving experience in anybody's book and whether it is the magnificent scenery and sunsets or just the everyday struggles of an ant for life and death, you will eventually ask yourself 'Why?' Your answers will be your own, and they will be many and varied. So it is wise to remember that although others will claim to have come very close to the answer, it's not the method that's important, it's getting to recognise the question in the first place. Although we paid few penalties for being 'outsiders' apart from in school, in other ways our lack of religion was tolerated extremely well and made no material difference to us at all. Habits and customs of a lifetime die hard in little forgotten corners of the world like this, and such incidents only serve to remind you of how a community can function as a whole when held together by a common thread. We were to become very familiar with such things as Stations (when Mass is said in a private house) and Wakes after the funerals and hopefully, in time to come, the attendance of heathens such as ourselves at functions like this will serve to make the

more zealous members of the community accept the fact that many 'outsiders' exist.

Continuing to pedal the eight miles twice a day to and from school, with breathing taking up most of my concentration and rendering me unable to take too much notice of my surroundings, it was only after several weeks' continual practice that I began to quite enjoy it – especially the homeward part which was mostly downhill. It was on one of these homeward journeys, weaving my way on a good freewheel section down through the woods with our bearded collie running on ahead of me that we first came in contact with a WILD animal. Not exactly a lion or a bear, but a huge dog fox which jumped out of the bank into the road, ending up nose to nose with Pepper.

It was hard to tell who was the most surprised, me, the fox or Pepper – both of which were much the same size. In those few frozen seconds of time you could almost see something in the depths of Pepper's surburban subconscious being dragged to the surface saying 'This is a fox. Dogs should chase foxes'. With a few more whirrs

and clicks of the old brain, he set off in pursuit. The fox
jumped smartly over the old stone wall on the opposite side
of the road and just stayed where he was crouched low in
the bracken. Pepper hurled himself over the wall (and the
fox) with a yelp and a crash, and his progress through
the undergrowth could be heard for several minutes later.
Meanwhile the fox looked at me and I looked at the fox.
Summoning up my best David Bellamy attitude and hoping
that it really was true that wild animals are more afraid of
you than you are of them, I remounted the rusty bike and
set hastily off.

The second confrontation required a little more courage
when just before breakfast one morning Casper refused to
come in and was seen to be barking his head off at a bush.
In actual fact it turned out that his attention was directed
at the other side of the bush and he was standing where he
was in the interest of self-preservation. Having examined
the bush thoroughly from all angles and stepping back to
get a better look at what could possibly be causing such an
outburst, my foot nearly came down fair and square on a
fully grown, very much alive, angry badger. Back round the
other side of the bush with Cassie, we peered through the
branches and reviewed the situation. The badger appeared
to be tangled up in the brambles which were wound round
her hind legs. Unable to understand why she couldn't pull
herself free, the awful truth that something would have to
be done to free her slowly dawned on me. Trying desperately
to remember all the teachings of my youth on the subject
in front of me, whilst the facts that they dug holes and
were supposed to spread TB seemed a little irrelevant, the
knowledge that they were fearsome fighters seemed very
much more to the point.

The logical answer was to hold her head in a forked
stick with one hand and free her with the other, but
there were a few minor setbacks to this plan, the first
being the small crowd of children who had gathered to

watch Mummy free the badger and the second was the extremely fearsome sharp teeth we were getting a good look at as she snapped repeatedly at anything coming too close. Of course, all of a sudden every forked stick in the area went missing, so taking the coward's way out and getting Markie to fetch the shears, we severed the brambles from their roots. Suddenly free, she made a dash for the gate and at once the reason for her predicament became obvious. Her back legs were paralysed, but dragging them behind her she set off down the road towards the woods. It seemed likely she must have been hit by a car and her chances of survival appeared very slim, but over the next year or so, on several occasions we noticed a badger hanging around the house. It never entered our minds that this could possibly be the same one until, early one morning, Pat went out through the porch to let the chickens out of their shed, and there in the cat-box with the cats was the badger. This time there were no snarls or bared teeth. She was obviously sick and very likely dying, and made no objections when Pat carried her in the box gently into a quiet corner of the big shed where later that day she died. From the old scars on her body we were able to identify her as that same paralysed badger of a year before. How she had survived all that time around our house and our own domestic animals' acceptance of her during that time was cause for wonder indeed.

There were to be many other occasions when we came into contact with the Big Wild Outdoors. We had the good fortune one day to find a whole school of pilot whales in the shallow warm water of a local cove. As the tide crept out we watched, horrified at the prospect of them being stranded, but all except one retreated to the deeper water some fifty yards out and waited there. One could only presume that the remaining one was sick as there seemed to be no external sign of injury. The whale was so close to shore that it would have easily been possible to reach out and touch it, especially at low tide when the water only came half way up its body. But it just lay there silent and still, perhaps reassured by the presence of the others waiting nearby. As the tide rose the others came to join the sick one again, but by that time it was getting too dark to see them clearly. Come morning they all had vanished back into the ocean. We were never to find out their reason for bringing that one whale into our sheltered bay, but the children and ourselves got a chance in a lifetime to see how these remarkable mammals show a caring and understanding for each other that many of our own species sadly lack.

We were to get glimpses of the beautiful, black shiny coat of the mink as they made forays to try and steal our eggs or chase the baby rabbits in the fields. Markie would pick up and bring home anything that stood still long enough for him to capture it and even one day took two large natterjack toads to a local funeral as he thought they would enjoy the experience. His obvious delight in birds and animals led to him come trotting along the beach one day with a rapidly decomposing otter that he had found half buried in the sand wrapped round his neck like a scarf. The surrounding occupants who had been sunning themselves were very thankful when a suitable grave had been dug several feet deep and Markie immersed repeatedly and thoroughly in the cold water to rid him of the smell.

He would weep buckets when even the smallest spider died and his sensitive nature led to our house becoming a sort of animal hospital. There were the injured seagulls found by the beach, baby rabbits dazzled by headlights, and lizards with no tails. A woodcock with a damaged wing spent time with us as well as endless baby birds that had fallen from their nests, so a rule had to be made that all such creatures, should they survive, must return from whence they came. But during the brief interlude they remained with us, we gained a little understanding of just

how many fascinating things are out there, if only we have the time to stop and see.

Once you get a little fitter from the constant pedalling and more confident, you will have time to start looking about you and notice (especially in autumn) the vast amount of wild fruits and berries in every hedgerow and common sense will tell you that as these are free and ripe, they should be in your kitchen. It is then time to mobilise your own personal picking team, ie the children. It is quite essential that when you start on something like the blackberries, you pick as many as you can as quickly as you can. The novelty of picking disappears along with about the second pound. It is also wise to remember that you will have at least one child who will put two blackberries in the bag and eat all the rest. He or she will then either be sick or refuse to walk home. There is one failsafe method you can employ at this time of year and that is each time one of them is disobedient, make the punishment of picking a pound of blackberries. This will do wonders for those autumn blues and bad tempers and go a long way to making the 70lb of jam needed for a year's supply. If you think 70lb of jam is exorbitant, think of one jar a week equalling fifty-two jars, all those jam roly-poly puddings and the snacks for a ten-year-old who is positively starving all of thirty minutes after a huge dinner. Whatever else you do, take at least three times as many bags as you think you need, because polythene bags are not very resistant to climbing through hedges.

Older children can be used to shin up trees and retrieve the wild plums that always hang enticingly out of reach or those clusters of scarlet berries on the rowan trees. Ignore any protests about how they are getting stabbed by the thorns on the sloe bushes. Believe me, little hands are much more deft at getting those sloes than your big ones. It is also wise to make sure you read the cookery book before setting out, because although rowan berries

are much easier to collect in vast quantities than sloes,
finding a use for 30lb of them stretches even the most
desperate of cooks. Rowan-berry jelly may taste excellent
with venison, but it doesn't taste so hot spread on school
sandwiches.

Having kept a close eye all through the spring and
summer on what is growing and ripening where, you will
eventually come to regard all the wild fruit growing in your
area as your own. You may well have been waiting for the
first frost to put the perfect bloom on your blue/black sloes,
only to find a tourist stop and pick the lot. I'm sure this is
how many of the local superstitions about lots of the fruit
and berries being poisonous arose and you will feel a little
foolish trying to tell some Frenchman in the middle of nowhere that this particular blackberry bush belongs to you.
So when you chance across a spot absolutely stuffed with
wild plums and the branches are groaning beneath their
weight, keep it to yourself and hope that thirty others are
not keeping the same secret. It also helps to carry a pair
of secateurs with you at all times and a rolled-up carrier
bag stuffed in your back pocket.

Listening to odd remarks dropped by others, such as a
tourist asking what all those lovely yellow mushrooms are,
can reveal hitherto unfound sources of goodies. Tourists
tend to ramble in places you wouldn't dream of going
and are a fund of information, if you can gently extract
it from them. Pat came home one day from the pub with
tales of these yellow mushrooms, which he surmised must
be chanterelles, and a very rough idea of their location,
which just happened to be in the depths of some very dense
forest. Bags were located, wellies put on, and off we went.
Being a sailor, Pat has an unerring sense of direction. Put
four trees around me and a few bushes and it could take
a search party several days to find me, so as the forest got
denser and denser, the thought that I might never see my
loved ones again got more and more prominent. Underfoot

grew every type of mushroom and toadstool known to man, except the yellow ones. Not everybody has a chance to see these from a bird's eye view, but as Pat insisted on doing his explorer-into-the-unknown bit, we were eventually reduced to crawling through the rhododendron thickets on our hands and knees. Even the dogs got fed up and went home. Just getting to the point of being too weak even to complain, we rounded another bush and there they were – a yellow carpet stretching as far as the eye could see. There wasn't a place to stand without crushing them, unless of course you stood on the footpath that ran alongside them on the neatly signposted 'tourist route'! But luckily nobody was passing to see these dishevelled, dirty explorers emerging from the bushes and we got ourselves enough chanterelles to last for a year.

A word of warning should be issued here to those of you to whom a mushroom is a little, white, round, button thing and that is never to eat any mushroom-like thing growing wild before taking absolutely expert advice. Even clutching an illustrated guide to mushrooms in one hand is of no real help. There is very little difference on first sight to the uninitiated between *Amanita phalloides* and *Amanita citrina*, but eating the former (the death cap) will probably kill you, whilst eating the latter (the false death cap) will just give you a nasty taste in your mouth. Chanterelles only have one real look-alike that isn't poisonous, and once you have picked a few thousand, even the children will learn to recognise them on sight. These can be successfully frozen and a corner found for them in your already bulging freezer.

We always made a point of explaining as best we could to the children the importance of never eating anything they found until they checked it was safe with us; in surroundings where every second bush is full of berries of some sort or other, this is a wise precaution. One warning that never occurred to us to give them was the danger of honey. Markie, then aged about four, knew that honey came from bees so he set off one day to get himself some. The fact that we didn't keep bees didn't deter him in the slightest, nor did the fact that bees and wasps look alike. He climbed up into the woods, found himself a wasps' nest hanging from a branch with wasps buzzing in and out and clobbered it with a stick. Being small, his stick hit the bottom of the nest, broke it open and the wasps fell down and swarmed on his head. Luckily, it was early November and the wasps were sleepy with the advent of winter, but in the few minutes it took me to locate his screams and reach him, his hair and face and clothes were covered with a thick layer of stinging insects. How none crawled into his open mouth is beyond comprehension, but clawing great handfuls of them off him seemed to take forever. Tearing his clothes off in an effort to get at the ones still stinging him inside his vest and pants and leaving a trail of these behind, somehow we got back down to the house where he was unceremoniously dumped in a cold water bath to try and alleviate the pain and drown any remaining wasps caught in his hair and round his body.

Later at the doctor's, with Markie looking as if he had just done three rounds with Muhammad Ali, we realised how lucky we had been that Markie wasn't allergic to the stings. What was also made obvious was the necessity of keeping a fully equipped first-aid box to hand in the house at all times. Although one of my main worries when we had first come to live so far away from 'civilisation' was what on earth would happen if we had an emergency, in reality you can cope with most things if you have a little knowledge, a few tools of the trade and you don't panic. Going so far as buying a large medical and first-aid book is a dubious advantage. Once, when Jason came home quite hysterical with an obviously broken collar bone, caused by parting company with his bike at great speed, he eventually was forced to stop crying and beg me to take him to the hospital because I was still leafing through the medical book trying to find the proper name for a collar bone and how it should be strapped up for the car journey. In desperation, we tied his arm to his body with a piece of rope to keep it still and although the doctor's eyebrows raised ever so slightly when we stumbled into casualty, it did actually work.

What is also well worth considering, which had never occurred to us, was what would happen if something were to happen to me? Happily worrying myself silly about how to protect the children from all these dangers that obviously lurked in the Great Wild Outdoors, my mind must have been elsewhere when my foot slipped, causing me to fall down the stairs just before giving the children tea one day. The loud crack my foot made on the way down was not as big a problem as staying conscious. The children, who were sitting at the table, had watched my descent with great curiosity and Jason thought it most strange to be told in no uncertain terms to empty a jug of cold water over my head until that great welcome dark painless place slipped far enough away. Although he was only five and our nearest neighbour lived over half a mile away, he set off with a torch in the pitch darkness to summon help. Everybody was quite marvellous and in no time at all the doctor arrived, strapping up my foot which was broken in several places and left me sitting in the middle of the living-room with the advice that there was no point going to the hospital until the swelling went down – in maybe three or four days – and then it could be X-rayed and plastered at the same time. As Pat was away of course when this happened, the thought of me sitting in the middle of the living-room for three or four days while the kids ran amok was altogether too much, so Grandma was phoned in England, Air Lingus alerted to my plight and the four of us flew back to stay with her whilst my foot recovered.

You may well be wondering why, when this accident

happened, we didn't phone for help instead of sending a small boy out into the dark. This was mainly because we didn't have a telephone. Our cottage may have had water and electricity, but other mains services that at one time we had taken so much for granted, were sadly lacking. After our first year we had come to recognise that life does not end if you don't have a telephone, and there are even the odd advantages like no telephone bills. But with the advent of my becoming a grass widow it did seem to be a practical advantage, so we filled out all the various forms and waited.

Two years and a great deal of money later we got our phone, and it was one of those marvellous black things with no numbers and a handle to wind. Discovering that we were disconnected at 6.00pm every night because we hadn't applied for Night Service was a bit of a setback, but this was eventually obtained and the bills could then start pouring through the door. When you cranked up the handle on the telephone you immediately became connected to Maureen at the local post office. Whoever the madman was that invented the subsequent digital phone system obviously never experienced the pleasure of having the wind-up variety. Combining an answering service second to none and a local information service that one could depend upon with unfailing certainty, it was a sad day when so-called 'progress' had us all converted to the new system.

Another missing mains service was any type of rubbish collection. Limited to town areas only, us country folks had to fend for ourselves. Anything burnable had to be burned in a home-made incinerator, anything compostable and inedible to chickens, ducks, geese, goats, etc was put on the compost heap and anything left, ie tins and bottles, had to be taken to the town dump on the weekly visit to the shops. As time passes, you can't help but notice that you will use less and less tins.

Tins become an expensive way of buying a lot of ruined food and a great deal of unwanted chemicals. Pre-packed, instant food is for those of us who haven't the time or the inclination to stop or to care. There is no mystic aura about cooking food the old-fashioned way and it doesn't take much longer than trying to fathom out the directions on a packet, but knowing what has gone into it does more for my peace of mind than any printed reassurances about lack of E numbers therein.

Luckily there seems to be a general leaning in the 'civilised' world towards greater awareness of what we put inside ourselves and this is projecting itself in the form of health food shops. Now, whilst we came very near to becoming vegetarians on many occasions due to our contact with animals, we never actually made the final step. But out here where one has the advantage of being able to 'do one's own thing', we were to come across many and varied ways of living amongst our friends and all of these, without exception, involved healthy eating. Whilst the children learned the lesson that anything new should at least be tried and experienced before writing it off, we became curious as to the possibility that they might just be right. The progression to such things as whole-wheat flour, the use of pulses and organically grown vegetables came easily and naturally, and as our vision increased with the looking, so our other senses grew simultaneously.

The scent of gorse flowers on a spring day so reminiscent of coconut, or that special smell of leaf mould in the woods in late autumn when the air is whirling with red and gold leaves replaced the dubious joys of carbon monoxide fumes and fresh air from an aerosol can. We became able to touch and feel and experience things in another world that had been there all the time, and except for a touch of Fate, might well have remained lost to us forever.

10

TAKE A DROP OF
SPARKLING WINE

In the early days of autumn, when the first storms herald-
ing the onset of winter made it impossible for Pat to go
out fishing and the boat was safely tucked in behind the
little stone bridge at Kilmakilloge out of the reach of the
pounding waves and flying spray, it was a bit like sharing
the same cage as a pride of restless lions. When two adults
and three growing children are all living in a tiny two-up
two-down cottage, these rainy days can become a nightmare, especially if one of them suddenly decides to paint
the living-room or build a goat-stand in the kitchen where
you are up to your elbows in chutney.

It was an occasion like this, when tempers were
beginning to get a touch frayed, that the suggestion was
made by me that they should all either go and pick some
blackberries or see who could be the first one to walk the
sixteen miles to Kenmare, or anything else that would take
a suitably long time and get them out of the house. Like a

flash, three hitherto noisy, complaining children suddenly became little angels deeply engrossed in a game of Ludo, whilst the Leader of the Pack, muttering things under his breath about how peaceful and quiet oil rigs were compared to here, flung on his coat, picked up a few carrier bags and left with the wind slamming the door for him. Three hours later he returned, very damp and muddy but with all his bad mood blown away by the wind and jubilantly plonked down three carrier bags full of blackberries on the kitchen table.

With growing amazement it dawned on me that his fisherman's instincts to empty the sea of fish, equally applied to land and, properly nurtured, could provide the 70lb of jam we needed each year with no trouble at all. No more days hassling the children to pick, not eat; no more scratched hands and purple fingers. The thought was quite marvellous and encouraged me to heap praise upon praise at the 23lb of blackberries and their collector. Of course, having to buy all the sugar with which to make the jam at one go made a bit of a hole in my limited housekeeping money, but that was a small fly in the ointment compared with my secret thoughts of directing all this picking energy in the right direction. By midnight all the jam was made and labelled, the kitchen cleaned up and bed was a very welcome sight.

Next morning, being dimly aware that Pat was up and gone very early, it seemed natural to presume that the weather had cleared enough for fishing. Like a steady drip of water, slowly my subconscious became aware of the lashing rain and the curtains moving in the draught where the windows didn't quite fit. 7.30am found me going through the usual daily motions of getting the troops up and dressed whilst simultaneously trying to remain asleep myself. By 8.00am, desperate for my morning cup of coffee and tottering half-awake into the kitchen, the sight of three more carrier bags full of blackberries confronted me, plus a wet, soggy, smiling, triumphant Pat. This was definitely not Plan A, or even Plan B, C or D. At this rate we would either overdose on blackberry jam or go broke from spending all our money on sugar and visions of all us slowly turning purple, just like the dear departed turkey, floated in front of me. With growing dismay my brain started dismally to wonder just how many pounds of blackberries there were in the whole of Ireland and whether it would be possible to direct his picking talents elsewhere. But discarding his muddy boots and wet clothes, he cheerfully informed me that this load was for wine.

Now, wine-making was totally unexplored territory for me, although we had experimented with several beer kits with some degree of success. Having had a pub before where one could have a drink whenever one felt the need, the enforced poverty of our new life had put a stop to all that. When you have only £28.00 a week to live on between five of you, spending over a pound on a pint of beer could well be grounds for divorce. Even with the advent of Pat's job on the rigs, it took us over two years to pay off all our long overdue debts and by the end of that time our previous need to have a drink the minute the sun passed over the yard-arm had long since disappeared. Budget upon Budget heaped taxes onto alcohol and prices soared to discourage us even further, but what we did miss was the chat and gossip and convivial atmosphere especially found in our local pub at Kilmakilloge.

To add insult to injury, oil rigs in the North Sea are 'dry', ie no booze and no women, although in recent years a couple have been known to splash out on the odd can of non-alcoholic lager at Christmas and an occasional visiting female geologist. For some reason best known to themselves, the oil companies think that showing non-stop blue movies is half the answer, and although one can quite willingly make up for that lack of foresight on his return, beer kits had to suffice for the other. But the rising prices at the pub had a secondary effect on the population. Instead of meeting there for a get-together, more and more people tended to meet in their homes and on more than one occasion we had been given a glass of home-made wine which ranged in taste from the pleasant to the almost impossible to swallow. So it was out with the self-sufficiency books again to see what they had to say about it.

Basically, after ploughing through all the instructions, it appeared that there were two ways of making wine: the hard way or the easy way, and there are no prizes for guessing which method we chose. With hindsight, it would be easier to describe the methods as either 'modern' or 'old fashioned'. The modern one uses all kinds of chemicals to make sure that every gallon of wine is perfect and it is fine if you are not bothered about what passes through you or remains inside. The old-fashioned way just uses fruit or flowers, water, sugar and yeast with maybe such things as the odd cup of tea thrown in to provide tannin if needed, or a handful of raisins for sweetness and colour. Whichever method you use, it is not the pastime for a budding alcoholic for, from the time you start to the time you finish and get to have a glass of it, is usually about a year.

But being ignorant of all these things and finding a recipe for blackberry wine therein, it didn't take me long to purchase all the necessary equipment and combine the ingredients. The resulting liquid looked something akin to purple mud and far from having any trouble getting it to ferment, it took me two days to clean up the mess in the airing cupboard where it had frothed right over the top of the bucket. But eventually all the sheets were re-washed and the fizzy mud poured into a demi-john and an airlock stuffed in the top to prevent further accidents. Every week for the next three or four months it was taken down and examined to see if it had cleared and turned into wonderful sparkling wine. It hadn't. After six months you still couldn't see daylight through the muddy contents, nor after eight, so it was decided to consult the bible and see what it said under the 'problems and cures' section.

Seemingly, all you had to do was add an egg white to the mixture and all would be well. But should the egg white be *au naturel* or whipped? It didn't say, so we decided to compromise and give it a bit of a beating. Frothy egg white added to purple mud gives you frothy purple mud and nothing else. It was also extremely difficult to fit this horrible frothy mixture back into the small opening at the top of the demi-john and, coming to the decision that this was the final straw, the whole lot got shoved right in the back of the airing cupboard whereupon we forgot all about it.

Three or four months later, it was probably the sight of the first blackberries in the hedges that jolted my memory about the wine and bringing the demi-john out into the light of day, there it was. A beautiful clear nectar fit for the gods with a taste surpassing even the finest Beaujolais – though perhaps we were just a touch biased in our opinions, especially after about the third bottle.

Flushed with success, this was to be the start of many a brew to come. Now more than ever, our year, instead of being divided into weeks and months, became regulated by the seasons. Spring would bring the yellow gorse flowers which are hell to pick, but make a super wine. You can also use the carpets of primroses which cover the fields down to the water's edge, or their friends and neighbours, the yellow dandelions which, according to my book, must only ever be picked on St George's Day. As this was also Mark's birthday and he didn't consider dandelion-picking much of a celebration, it tended to get left to the next day or the next day after that. This could be why the dandelion wine was never a great success. Then there is wine made from hawthorn blossom (which is almost as hazardous to pick as the gorse flowers), or the lovely creamy heavily scented elder flowers. You only need twelve elder flowers for a gallon of wine and they must be picked on a warm sunny day, but make sure you never carry them home in the car with the windows shut, because their heavy scent has the effect of dulling the reactions.

Whilst you are up a tree picking the elder flowers, it's well worth picking another few and having a go at making elder-flower champagne, though it's wise not to make too much. This is because it takes one day to make, sits around for only two weeks and it all has to be drunk by the end of the third week. This means that in the space of just one week, you may have to drink five gallons of it and unless the weather is glorious and you can invite thirty people over to lie in the sun and get incoherent on elder-flower champagne, you have major problems. After the third week it just goes on getting fizzier and fizzier, then the bottles start to explode and it always seems such a shame to pour it down the drain.

Summer brings the gooseberry champagne which has much the same effect, but this can be stored in proper champagne bottles and, with correct wiring, will keep indefinitely. Then there's wine made from parsley, blackcurrants and redcurrants (the former delicious drunk hot on a winter's evening), honeysuckle and plums, rose petals, peaches and my most favourite summer wine, meadowsweet. Collecting the meadowsweet flowers on a hot summer's day is a pleasure kept under wraps for myself alone. The memory of lying stripped off in a bank of meadowsweet, getting toasted by the sun and watching the insects drowsily buzzing around overhead amongst the frothy heads of the flowers against a deep blue sky, will remain with you even on the darkest winter days when you sip this wine. It contains the very essence of summer in each delicious drop. In autumn, along with the blackberries, there are damsons and elder-berries, if you can get to them before the birds do, raspberries and

sloes. In the waysides crabapples and rosehips are ripening towards winter when, if you have any demi-johns left at this stage, you can experiment with orange, almond and coffee wines.

The only really important thing to remember when wine-making is that you cannot speed up the process without the chemicals. If you want a really natural wine, you just have to wait until every grain of sugar has been turned into alcohol by the yeast and all fermentation has ceased. It is quite difficult for the amateur to judge this point because if the room where the demi-john is located gets colder with the onset of winter, sometimes the wine will appear to have stopped fermenting and look quite clear and ready to be bottled. So having got it all corked and labelled, it will then secretly start fermenting again, just a little, but enough for one sunny day to bring the whole thing to a climax and send the cork shooting out of the bottle.

We had stored all our bottles on their sides in the living-room in some wine racks that Pat had made over the piano and one particularly chilly evening in late January,

having a good natter with friends after an equally good dinner, Pat stoked up the fire to make us all cosy and warm. Unfortunately it also warmed up the bottles and without warning one of them suddenly shot out its cork and a great fountain of fizzy blackberry wine emptied over the heads of our guests. It therefore is probably a better idea if you store the bottles in some cool, dark place – like a shed or a garage or a larder, if you are lucky enough to have one.

As you will have long since reached the stage when it becomes a choice of the sheets or the wine in the airing cupboard, you can always stand the demi-johns on the windowsills or shelves of a warm sunny room. The soft sound of bubbles rising through the airlocks will become as familiar to you as the chatter of the children's voices. For people with husbands like mine, you can also resort to five-gallon containers or even a barrel in desperation. All you have to do is spend a year without drinking a drop and the following year you can begin. On the basis of safety in numbers, we experimented with many different varieties the first couple of years, making just a gallon of each until we settled on about half a dozen that we really liked and then just made those in bulk, although to start with not every wine was a roaring success.

The self-sufficiency books will warn you about the dreaded vinegar fly and how it only needs one corpse floating around at any stage of your wine-making to render the whole lot undrinkable. You may have never noticed these little chaps hanging around before, but believe me, you only have to pick up your demi-john to become engulfed in a whole swarm of them. But even if the odd one does meet his Maker in your wine, whatever you do, don't throw the wine away because it's very easy to turn it into the most marvellous vinegar. Just throw a bottle of ordinary malt vinegar in the demi-john, empty the sour wine on top of it, shake the whole lot up, then put a bit of gauze over the top of it and put the entire thing in the back of a hot press to keep it nice and warm. Whatever you do don't look at it for three months because the sight of wine turning into vinegar is not a pleasant one and is quite likely to put you off ever using it. But in three months the nasty bits will have all sunk to the bottom and you will be left with a gallon of clear and very tasty wine vinegar.

But what to do with three or four gallons of wine vinegar is the problem. The answer is simple. Use the red variety to make pickles and chutneys and the white or rosé for herb and flower vinegars which make marvellous Christmas presents for everybody and are quite delicious used in dressings for salads. Whilst poking around in The Pantry one day (our local health food shop), there in front of me was a bottle of tarragon vinegar which was twice the price of ordinary vinegar. Ok, so it looked pretty, but a close examination of the bottle and the contents revealed that it was just a sprig of tarragon stuck inside a bottle of vinegar, and the two things we were not short of were herbs and vinegar. On getting home the children were offered a penny for each empty small Lucozade bottle they could find and bring to me intact and then, having cleaned and sterilised each bottle, it was only necessary to push in the herbs and top up the whole thing with vinegar.

Whilst I was doing this, Pat was occupied with building more shelves in the porch, as the bottles need to sit in a nice sunny place for the whole summer to ensure that the vinegar takes up all the flavour. It was also quite fascinating to watch how the vinegar changed to the colour of what was in it, though with herbs this does tend to be various shades of purple as the flowers of such things as sage, marjoram and thyme are all this colour. Just out of curiosity to see if it worked with other things, we tried mixing the vinegar with honeysuckle, marigolds, pink and red rose petals, rosehips and blackberries, elder flowers and meadowsweet till the shelves of bottles were every colour of the rainbow. Each fruit or flower stays perfectly preserved in the vinegar for all time and if you then consult a good herb book you can find out the old-fashioned properties of the herbs, fruits and flowers and write these upon the labels: tansy vinegar for easing toothache; pennyroyal dabbed on the odd spot of leprosy; and how sage vinegar does wonders for the plague. You can even use the rose-petal vinegar as a skin astringent if you don't want it in the salad or just leave any of the bottles sitting in a sunny place oblivious of the frost outside to remind you of the warm, sunny blissful days of summer.

Pat took as much interest as me in the making of all these things and would hunt around book shops on his way home from the rig for books with new recipes or methods of making things. As a result, the children were surprised suddenly to find themselves getting home-made fruit syrups to drink for their school lunches. These can be made from rosehips which are bursting with vitamin C, blackberries, blackcurrants, raspberries or even strawberries. A bottle of home-made fruit syrup will dilute down to give twice as many drinks as one purchased from a shop, and for less than half the price.

But despite the increase in our production, we still seemed to have an excess of fruit each year, especially sloes, so the answer seemed to be sloe gin and other such liqueurs. These are basically gin, fruit and sugar mixed together and abandoned for three or four months. Even buying it duty free on Pat's way home, the fact of actually pouring two pints of gin into a kilner jar of sloes definitely seemed something close to a sin, despite the delicious end result. So it was decided to experiment with a certain illicit Irish spirit and this worked just as well and was considerably cheaper.

Unlike the wines and vinegars, instead of requiring somewhere sunny, the liqueurs needed a cool, dark place. As they also improved considerably with age, this place had to be hidden well away from secret samplers and the like where they could remain undisturbed. As any mother knows, such places don't exist in a house full of children unless bolted, barred and sealed with several strong padlocks. Nowhere really suitable came to mind until one day, whilst dusting the old upright piano, the front fell off. There among the pedals and the wires was the perfect place to stash the bottles. For several years to come, having made say four bottles, two were put in the cupboard and two stashed away in the piano – the latter known only to me. The children's legs were not long enough to reach the pedals and all would have remained undisturbed if it hadn't been for the arrival of the piano tuner late one night.

Because the poor old piano had seen better days, some two years previously Pat had happened to mention to the manager of one of the hotels in Kenmare that we needed a piano tuner. Like many things in Ireland, you may think they are long forgotten, but in truth they just take a while to get around to doing anything and the fact that it was two years later and eleven o'clock at night didn't deter him one bit. Before I could leap to their rescue, your man had sat down at the piano and embarked on a bit of a tune. He obviously was a little surprised at the percussion that accompanied him as bottle rocked against bottle and even more surprised to find me grovelling around at his feet emptying out my secret stash. But obviously a true Irishman, he took it in excellent humour, especially when Pat suggested that we might all have a wee tasting session, and piano tuning was abandoned for another day.

It perhaps would be worth mentioning at this point some of the other hazards of wine-making that befell us in those early days. As we experimented with wine after wine, many people got to know of our efforts and indeed got to sample a few as well. As our stocks increased we could afford to be generous when filling up the glasses and many a happy hour was passed with the guests eventually departing with a slight list to starboard in the early hours.

I acquired a certain 'reputation' as a wine-maker and we would often return home to find little thank-you presents left on the doorstep. Such things as baskets of apples or a box of rotten bananas with a little note to the effect that they looked forward to sampling the end result the next year. Whereas one would normally have slung the lot, their kindness made me feel duty bound to see what could be salvaged and have a go at making the wine – often it was well worth the trouble.

Grandma had made yet another useful present to us: this time an electric juice extractor which cut down the initial hard work to great effect. Amongst other things, we used this to have a go at making cider one year when apples were so plentiful that you couldn't give them away, and although the end result was so sour that it brought tears to the eyes, it packed a punch that you would remember for several days afterwards.

On my various cycling expeditions, a mental note would be taken of what was growing where and then when it was ripe, and I would set off in the car with collecting bags and secateurs to harvest the crop of berries, flowers, etc. Unbeknown to me, it was these little expeditions, sometimes involving climbing fences, crossing fields or struggling through hedges, that was to culminate in my opening the front door one afternoon to half a dozen extremely fierce-looking, uniformed and plain-clothed police officers. Brandishing a search warrant they rushed in, pushed us all into one room and one stood guard at the door while the others searched the house and lands. Somewhat taken aback and at a loss for an explanation to give the children, it was not until they came to question us that a little light was thrown on the situation. Apparently they had been staked out hidden in the bushes around a field in which was growing a large crop of marijuana, waiting for whoever planted it to show up. And guess who came along, struggled through the bushes, waded waist deep through the 'grass' and re-emerged carrying several bulging carrier bags? None other than me.

At first they were not inclined to believe my story that the bags were filled with rowan berries, but a quick trip to the kitchen revealed the loot still in the process of being washed in the sink and shaking their heads in total disbelief, they returned to their bushes. We did hear later, via the extremely reliable bush telegraph that, having spent several hours searching our house and lands, when they returned to the field in question all the marijuana was harvested and gone.

Having spent six years without ever drinking any shop-bought wine, Pat decided to give me a treat and to take me out to a posh restaurant in Kenmare for my fortieth birthday. Being able to choose anything that took my fancy from the menu was a great treat, and to accompany the delicious meal he selected a bottle of extremely expensive French white wine. A few sips confirmed that it tasted lovely and we were all set for a truly romantic evening. By the end of the starter course my face was flushed and my body was feeling very hot. Having only drunk a quarter of a glass of wine it didn't seem possible that could be to blame. Maybe it was just the crowded restaurant and still air.

Taking refuge in the powder room halfway through the main course and dabbing my face with cold water, the only explanation seemed to be some terrible illness that had suddenly struck me down without warning. The sweat was pouring off me, my face was bright red and it took a great effort of will-power on my part not to be sick. Getting a grip on myself and reluctantly returning to the table, it was the sight of the arrival of the birthday cake, made specially for me by the restaurant with layer upon layer of whipped cream, raspberries and meringue aglow with candles, that finally did me in. Just able to gasp to Pat to take me out immediately, he managed to steer me into the car-park and the bushes before I was horribly and thoroughly sick. As we had both eaten the same meal and he was fine, the doctor diagnosed an allergic reaction and with a bit of investigation we discovered that many French white wines have a histamine added as a preservative and it was this that had triggered off such a violent reaction in me. It seemed that my prolonged absence from shop-bought wine and additives had caused the allergy to these particular ones, so I would have to exercise a great deal more care in the future – although it did have the effect of making us wonder what all those additives in food do to you, once your system has become immune.

With the passing of time, people have got to know me and my peculiar little ways and more of them are taking the time to ramble the highways and byways and get pleasure from all the different kinds of flowers and fruits that are there for the taking. In these days of instant everything and constantly rising prices, you will be quite amazed at how much pleasure you will get from a bowl of wild plums or blackberries in the depths of winter or what conviviality there is in just a drop of sparkling wine.

11

NON-RETURNABLE US

There will come a time after a while when you will have visitors to stay and you will invariably be asked the question 'What on earth do you find to do all day?' Try to restrain the urge to hit them. They are merely presuming that because you live in such a beautiful place, life is one constant long holiday and surely you should have become bored with all that enforced idleness by now? Instead, send them out to milk the goat, or if that fails to impress try a brisk five-mile walk over the mountainside to look for that elusive nest where the ducks are laying out. It the exercise doesn't finish them off, then the large dosage of fresh air will.

Without you saying one single word, they will find out just how wrong all that media coverage was of what one should wear in The Country these days. Tweeds and a nice silk blouse are just not quite right for scrambling through the occasional hedge or wading through a swollen stream, and gin and tonics before dinner on the porch aren't quite the same when you're being stared at by a hungry goat.

The real trick is to say absolutely nothing and just sit back mentally and watch them 'adapt' to what country life is really all about. We always say that any visitor must stay at least a week, for it will take them that long just to un-wind and stop rushing around mentally and physically in ever decreasing circles.

Children visiting come into a different category alto-gether. Compared with what the majority of them are used to, life down here amongst the yokels is pure bliss. The variety that are used to having to change their clothes at least three times a day in case they should get them dirty, usually run completely amok. The rest, having got over their fear of the animals and rushing indoors each time it starts to rain, will settle in with no trouble at all, and by themselves, could remain indefinitely. But the visit of the grown-ups should be no longer than two weeks at the most, because by that time they will be making ominous mutterings about abandoning everything back home and coming to live near you.

At this point it is worth mentioning to them that there are four different possibilites to be considered when getting away from it all. The first is that, presuming they have a great deal of money, they can buy a number of acres of good arable land and a house and set about the full-blown self-sufficiency bit in earnest. At least it will give the locals some chance of employment. If on the other hand they are not rich, but have some talent that will enrich not only themselves, but others, they can work from home and make up for lack of income with State help. By talent, one implies that this means such things as art, pottery, weaving, stonemasonry, carpentry, etc, etc. It is the influx of such people that has brought the pattern of life here full circle and their ability to live alongside the locals instead of trying to impose outside influences on them, has greatly enriched both sides of the coin.

Their third possibility is to be like us, with one partner

becoming a grass widow or widower and the other engaged
in full-time employment elsewhere. As they won't be able
to afford two houses, this does have the disadvantage that
the employment has to be live-in. In an industry, such as
the oil industry, which is reputed to have the highest divorce rate in the world, this does require the co-operation
of two mule-headed individuals who care and trust each
other enough to be able to live apart at times and still make
it work. The fourth possibility is a non-starter, which is
to live entirely on the State. Those who think they can
come and live away from it all and do absolutely nothing
except collect the dole, are kidding themselves. If they
don't freeze or starve to death first, they are more likely to
go absolutely and completely nuts. The common idea that
areas like this are peopled with hippies who spend all day
in a drug-induced trance is rubbish. Although in summer
time one does get the occasional influx of Beautiful People
with their minds on Higher Things, I've yet to meet one
that survived six months of an Irish winter without a wee
touch of reality creeping in.

If they don't fall into one of these first three categories, the
chances of survival are very slim for any extended period.
It should also be mentioned that if children are involved
in the move, they must be young enough to adapt to the
new way of life, new schools, etc. It's no good taking a
teenager who's used to discos, piles of friends and the
latest trendy clothes and expecting them to understand the
joys of self-sufficiency. The parents must also be of an age
where they can cope reasonably without any mains services
and must be of a disposition whereby they don't spend the
whole day comparing what they've got with what they left
behind. Any potential settlers should be quite clear that just
because you are so content with your way of life, it does
not mean that things such as arguments, bad tempers and
moods no longer exist and that everything is beautiful and
serene. Pat and I still have some real humdingers of rows,

ending up with one of us stamping our feet and marching out of the door. The trouble is that once outside, there isn't much place to go and certainly no one to tell and kicking the goat is no help at all. So you do have to learn to say sorry rather more quickly than usual, unless you want to spend the rest of your life in the chicken shed.

There will be as many bad days as good days. Changing your environment doesn't immediately change your character. Only time can do that. If you were miserable together before you moved, believe me, isolation is no cure. All self-sufficiency will achieve is to show you just how deficient in the ways of life you are.

After some time has passed in your attempt to be, or not to be, self-sufficient, the opportunity will arise for you to return to 'civilisation' and you are then bound to ask yourself if you have done the Right Thing. This, naturally, will depend on your own particular circumstances, but a few things are likely to come as a bit of a shock and it is wise to be prepared for them.

The first overwhelming impression will be that you have been suddenly struck down with a severe case of agoraphobia, particularly if your place of entry happens to be, as ours was, Heathrow Airport, although any large town or city or main railway station would do just as well. All the common symptoms of this disease, such as agitation, sweating and rapid pulse will be brought on by just the sheer volume of people around you. Being questioned in depth by customs because you don't happen to know exactly where to go and because they take your terrified pallor as a sure sign of guilt will not help, neither will generally being pushed and pulled in all directions.

But if you think this is bad, just wait till you go out onto the motorway. Whatever else happens, don't attempt to drive. Six lanes of cars hurtling suicidally in two directions, regardless of anything or anybody, will be an amazing shock to the system. Somebody lurking in the approach road, white with terror and doing three miles per hour will not be appreciated by the general public and abusive language and honking horns will do nothing to effect a quick cure. If you can travel all the way into London with your eyes shut, take a taxi and hang the expense. Whatever else happens don't open them till you have reached your destination. Just try to breathe deeply, hang on and think of other things.

Of course, you can always take the subway or a train. Unlike the place you have just left, it is important to remember never to get cheerfully into your seat and say hello to everyone around you, pass your sweeties around and ask to borrow someone's magazine. And whatever else happens, never make eye-contact with anyone. If you do so people will start to regard you as a probable sex maniac, or mistake you for a foreigner and start to make whispered comments about your clothes. No matter how carefully you have dressed, you can be quite sure that you will be at least four years out of date and you will be the only person in the entire carriage who looks like an ageing maiden aunt. The fact that every female appears to be wearing a ritual mask of make-up and their head has obviously been dragged through a hedge backwards at speed, should be studiously ignored.

If you want to be totally and expertly embarrassed, take the children with you. No amount of pre-trip organisation with lists of do's and don'ts will have any effect on them at all. It will be like throwing them into the middle of Disney World and Star Wars all at once. Having spent years impressing upon them that they should always tell the truth in an open and frank manner, a running questionnaire on why the girl sitting opposite has green and orange hair and is that one next to her a man or a woman or are the couple in the corridor making babies will not have everybody in uproarious laughter. You will get several seats to yourself and once they are vacated, nobody else will sit

there as they will assume you have some catching disease or a nasty smell.

If the worst should come to the worst and you have to travel before you have managed to save up the air fare, there is always the coach or, in our case, the boat. To be deliberately confined in a small space with a great many other people for anything up to a day is only for the hardened traveller and it is guaranteed to ruin any holiday you might have had in mind. It's possible that you might catch a glimpse of how it is supposed to be if you are rich enough to travel first class, but anything else is somewhat reminiscent of steerage class on a nineteenth-century ship being taken forcibly to the penal colonies. The prospect of adding to this nightmare by taking the children with you is alarming and should only be undertaken in situations of dire emergency. Children need to be got from a to b in the shortest possible time, unless you are prepared to cope with the muck, the tantrums, the sulks and the sick.

Having arrived at your destination, you will then have to explain (if you can) why they are not allowed to walk on the grass, pick up things and have a look at them in shops, say hello to strangers in the street, wave to passing cars, go out on their own, etc, etc, etc. You will see that for them it is like being placed in Fairyland and not allowed to touch. Don't worry, disillusion will soon set in. They will eventually tire of twenty-four-hour-a-day television and being confined to the house. If you just hold on a bit, even a five-year-old will soon realise that he or she is no longer free. All this glitter and gaudy magic, this world of non-stop rush, coloured lights and empty dreams will pale beside the elation of climbing a tree and leaning out of the top-most branch, master of all they survey.

This does not mean, however, that you should deprive them of the opportunity to see for themselves. We have found the best way is to tie a large label round their neck, donate them to Air Lingus as an 'unaccompanied child' and send them, one at a time, to stay with Grandma. Here they can stay for a week, be spoiled rotten and taken to all those places you wouldn't dream of going and then be returned to you in a similar manner. You can start doing this from about the age of four, but any child under that age is best left at home if you really do want a holiday.

People often ask us where we go on holiday and are somewhat surprised to find that we don't. If you happen to live in one of the most beautiful parts of the world, by the sea and amongst the mountains, it seems a little odd to us to want to go elsewhere. It is possible, however, to appreciate that some people need to take the odd break from self-sufficiency in order to recharge themselves. It can do wonders for making you appreciate just how much you have got, as well as giving you a chance to enjoy some of the things that are not available to those who live away from it all, such as the theatre, the cinema and the arts.

One of the other things that will strike you and the children on your trips back to so-called 'civilisation' is what a throw-away society it all is. Jason once spent two weeks in Dublin whilst the other two children recovered from whooping cough and, when asked on his return what wonderful things he had seen on his first trip to a big city, was heard to remark about how much rubbish there was all over the place. Having no mains services is a great way to learn to be tidy and make full use of everything to hand. We never throw away a single carton, jam jar or bottle. Everything is hoarded away ready to be put to some other use and each plastic bag is washed out, dried and put away to be used again. Once you realise that what you throw away is quite likely to show up again in your drinking water, you become a little bit more careful what you discard and where you put it.

If you have to fix your own washing machine, you tend to treat it with a little extra TLC and it's quite amazing how having to repair your own car makes you service

it regularly. Having learned the hard way and taken my three, very small, darlings back to England on two occasions shortly after we settled in here, I then became firmly resolved never to repeat the mistake of travelling *en famille* and apart from them having the odd holiday on their own, we stayed where we were.

This, of course, did not apply to Pat who continued living his schizophrenic existence travelling between his rig and our home. This normally meant a two-day travelling experience to and from Aberdeen on each end of his work hitch. At the end of this time he was so exhausted that he never really wanted to discuss the joys of life on an oil rig and was content to spend his time off forgetting all about it. So things continued until one day his rig came down to drill a hole just off the south coast of Ireland and from being totally ignorant of the world of the oilman, it was suddenly Dallas for real in the living-room. Although he worked in the office in Cork during the rig's stay in Irish waters, he was the only member of the crew or staff that actually lived here and the temptation to bring them all home with him and show them what they were missing proved too great. Suddenly we were awash with cowboy boots, studded belts and soft Yankee drawls as they expressed their appreciation of the incredible scenery, the home cooking and the general laid-back way of life compared to the rig.

The children were most impressed by their multi-purpose watches and fast cars, and doubly so when Pat's boss actually left his Mazda RX7 with me for four months because he had plenty of other cars back in Cork and Aberdeen. Whilst doing absolute wonders for the old ego, its ground clearance and petrol consumption left a lot to be desired. Then, just before the rig pulled anchors to return to the North Sea, by way of a thank-you present the office arranged for me to be taken out to the rig for the day.

At this stage, having not been back to any kind of civilisation for nearly five years, the thought of a day on

an oil rig as the only female with eighty men, the majority of whom had been out there for nearly a month already, was a touch alarming. How would my fear of heights be in a helicopter and what did one wear to be correctly dressed on oil rigs? The latter was jeans and an anorak, and the former was overcome by the pattern of events. Firstly, in order to travel in a helicopter, you have to wear a survival suit. This day-glo orange rubbery marvel covers even your feet and renders you totally sexless. This might have something to do with the fact that the small size had a crutch that hung round my knees, all kinds of pockets, gloves and lumps and that one then had to put a life-jacket on top of the whole ensemble. To add insult to injury, once you have struggled into all this lot, they then put you and your luggage onto a giant pair of scales and weigh you in front of everybody.

Then you go out to the helicopter, trying to run whilst at the same time ducking under the whirling rotor blades and clinging on to all those bits of you that are in danger of being blown off. Inside, it's like being all wedged together

in a giant sardine can with rotor blades rendering all conversation impossible. To get some relief from the noise, you are provided with ear muffs, through which you can either hear piped music or the pilot explaining in depth about what to do when you come down into the water. My attention was distracted at this point by the fact that we then taxied out onto the runway like a plane. About to try and complain to Pat that it was no different to an ordinary plane, she suddenly rose vertically into the air, leaned forward a bit and off we went. With her large windows and a cloudless blue sky, the conditions were ideal for the quick forty-five minute trip to the rig, though my first sight of this metal monstrosity was slightly alarming.

She was enormous, taller than the Eiffel Tower, rising out of the water on four giant legs. It seemed impossible that being a semi-submersible she was actually floating on giant pontoons under the water. A chance at a better view came when the pilot announced that as they had a female on board, he would do a couple of circuits of the rig so I could take some photos and it was not until later that the realisation hit me that we must have been completely tipped on our side to do this. My fear of heights didn't actually come into play until we landed on a large flat area called the helideck, having descended far too close for my liking to the tall tower bit. Still clutching my shoes and unable to even scream above the noise of the rotor blades, it appeared that one was supposed to run right off the side of the deck. All the walkways were like strong chicken wire and gave you an uninterrupted view straight down the hundred or so feet into the heaving water below. If it hadn't been for Pat pushing me from behind and a sudden overwhelming instinct for self-preservation, my entire day would have been spent face down on the helideck without ever seeing inside.

It had been announced on the Tannoy system to one and all that there was a female aboard, although they might just as well have announced that there was a visiting Martian. Having struggled out of the somewhat sweaty survival suit and taken straight to the canteen for some coffee, this 'female' was immediately put on display to one and all. Instead of the wolf-whistles or lewd remarks that others perhaps a touch younger than me sometimes have to put up with, it was the total silence that was unnerving. Everybody just stopped where they were and stared. In the canteen every sip of coffee that passed my lips was watched closely by everybody and I felt considerable relief when Pat took me on a trip round the rig.

Once you step outside, everybody has to wear a hard hat with their name on. Mine said 'Brian' in large black letters, which prompted the occasional remark as to just how successful the operation must have been. The one thing you don't get to see on an oil rig is oil. Every bit is gleaming clean and, like Alice, you seem to have shrunk in comparison to the giant-sized hooks and bolts and chains everywhere. Inside is a world without windows like a stainless steel air-conditioned rabbit hole, whilst outside the noise is continuous and unending. This is no Wonderland though, it's a world of hard work on long shifts with very little to break the monotony. A world that gives no leeway to the pounding of the seas or to the difference between day and night. You work, you eat, you sleep, day after day in unending wearisome sameness. It's no place for emotions or feelings and the sudden presence of a female in this place only serves to remind the men of what and where they are. The helicopter trip home serves as a bridge between illusion and reality, although it is only possible for me now to appreciate just why some of the men after a period of time have trouble telling which is which.

My trip out to the rig came as a gentle reminder to me of just how governed by the length of daylight hours and the seasons our life had become, instead of by the clock. We thought nothing of going to bed at 9.30 each

night and rising again at 7.00am. Any notions you might have of planning each day are impossible. By the time you are through seeing to the children and the animals each morning, it's either time for lunch or tea. There have been occasions when it was necessary for me to spend up to two days hopelessly looking for a lost duck, or five hours on a windswept mountainside trying to figure out just where the passing cow stood on our water pipe. You end up with a rough list of jobs to be done in the darker recesses of your mind and just cope with the more important of these that are necessary for your survival the following day.

It's probably the unexpected nature of each day that makes life so full and interesting. There's never time to stop and feel fed up or lonely. Even as a grass widow, loneliness very rarely catches me unawares, having got into the habit of getting on with all my little projects whilst Pat is away, so that on his time home we can take it relatively easy. The only thing missing is lack of adult conversation at times. Discussing the merits of the flying abilities of purple dragons as opposed to green ones, doesn't stretch the intellect to great lengths and one does tend to talk to oneself a lot. But the quiet times make up for all this. Living away from it all, being self-sufficient or whatever, without all the accepted hustle and bustle of everyday life, you get the added bonus of Space and Time. The Space can be anything, anywhere or anytime, but it's a pause in the headlong rush of life from birth to death. A pause where you can stop and reflect, gather your wits around you, open your eyes and ears and take note. With no outside influences to push or pull you, you get the Time to find your own direction and, with luck, a little certainty that it is the right one. Being a grass widow taught me to stand on my own two feet and to reach the inevitable conclusion that women are just as good as men in every way. I'm no great women's libber even now and still am not sure that women should or will rule the world, but we do have a place on an even footing. It's just all a question of balance.

Part of this balance is learning to live alongside all different kinds of people and not to be too fussy about them just in case they treat you the same way. You will meet the weird and the wonderful, the religious and the fanatics, the super-efficient, the muddlers and the no-hopers, but they are all held together by a common thread and that is the need to survive. Whether you are surviving against the elements, or just lack of money becomes immaterial. In such a society there is no class barrier or age barrier. They are as irrelevant as they are artificial. Nobody gives a damn whether your house is tidy or if your car is clean. Suddenly you are being taken for who you are and not for what you are. And finding out just who you are and if you like yourself or not, can be quite fascinating. So can any improvement or change you fancy making. Total self-sufficiency is an impossibility. There are not enough hours in the day, enough strength in your muscles or enough money in the kitty to make it work. The only possible way it can ever begin to come about is with a commune of people all living and working together, but then that presents untold problems just by its very nature. You just have to realise that you are going to be deficient in many ways physically and mentally. There are going to be certain things that you can't live without and things that by their very nature make life a lot simpler. Self-sufficiency or self-deficiency must be, therefore, a state of mind, not of being. If that moment ever comes when you can reach the end of just one day and be perfectly satisfied, perfectly content, then believe me, you have arrived.